WINNING WAYS

IN

COMMERCIAL

REAL ESTATE

**18 Successful Women Unveil the
Tips of the Trade in the Real Estate World**

Also by Splendor Publishing

The Art & Science of Loving Yourself First
'cause Your Business Should Complete You Not Deplete You!

25 Brilliant Business Mentors:
Their Top Tips to Catapult You to Success

The Happy Law Practice:
Expert Strategies to Build Business
While Maintaining Peace of Mind

The Influential Entrepreneur:
Position Yourself for Win-Win Engagement

Out-of-the-Box Marketing & Promotion
For Interior Designers and Decorators

Accessorizing for Design Professionals

Moneytudes

WINNING WAYS

IN

COMMERCIAL REAL ESTATE

18 Successful Women Unveil the
Tips of the Trade in the Real Estate World

Compiled by Pamela J. Goodwin

Co-authored by:

Linda Alexander   Lynn Dowdle   Brenda Ford
Pamela J. Goodwin   Jessica L. Herrera   Donna Johnson
Gwen MacKenzie   Jennifer K. Pierson   Valerie Richardson
Alice Seale   Karla Smith   Karin E. Sumrall
Jill Szymanski   Harriet Tabb   Liz Trocchio-Smith
Lisa Walker   Tina Wolfe

Chapter 18 by an Anonymous
Commercial Real Estate Professional

Splendor Publishing
College Station, TX

SPLENDOR PUBLISHING
Published by Splendor Publishing
College Station, TX.

First published printing, July, 2014

Library of Congress Control Number: 2014942760
Winning Ways in Commercial Real Estate: 18 Successful Women
Unveil the Tips of the Trade in the Real Estate World
1. Business 2. Reference

ISBN-10:1940278090
ISBN-13:978-1-940278-09-4
Business/Reference

Printed in the United States of America.

Cover Background: 38037883 Thatpichai | Dreamstime

For more information, or to order bulk copies of this book for events,
seminars, conferences, or training, please contact
SplendorPublishing.com.

Dedication

This book is dedicated to all the ambitious and hard-working women in commercial real estate who are determined to make a difference and to inspire the next generation entering the field.

"There is no elevator to success. You have to take the stairs."
-Unknown author

Contents

Chapter 1

Getting Started: Learn About Yourself and Keep Correcting Course
by Linda Alexander

Certain events and principles made a difference in my life. I experimented with several jobs to determine what kind of work I was suited to. I had the courage to take an occasional leap like moving across the country or changing careers. Persistence and obtaining a good education allowed me to succeed. I try to be diligent and professional at work. I think it is critical to be ethical and polite when dealing with others.

I have lived in Texas all of my adult life. Through my work I have been fortunate to see cities all around the country. I grew up in a suburb of Los Angeles. My father died when I was seven and I was raised by my mom; a well-traveled, interesting, enthusiastic school teacher. My grandmother lived with us. My aunt, uncle, and cousins were always close by. It was a very supportive middle class environment.

College was an expectation. I finished the last two years of my undergraduate degree at Texas Christian University in Fort Worth near my father's family.

My life seemed quite unremarkable until I went out into the world and saw how many people lacked support from their family. I realized what an advantage that foundation gave me.

The women on both sides of my family were nurses and teachers. Since just listening to tales from the hospital made me feel sick, I knew I could not be a nurse. A summer teaching job at a nursery school (alone with twenty-eight three year olds) proved to be a humbling, nerve-racking experience. My first summer job had revealed my dislike for clerical work. It was fortunate that I learned this at the earliest possible moment. Many young women take clerical positions and find it very difficult to ever move out of them. Now I knew what I couldn't do and while there were other careers left to choose from, I just didn't know what they were.

I didn't think any undergraduate college degrees would really prepare me for a profession except maybe nursing or accounting (I would since add other things to that list). I observed my aunt who was the dean of the nursing school at TCU and the president of the National League for Nursing. She was likeable with a ready smile, analytical, articulate, and hardworking as well. She succeeded because of these qualities. My aunt was in a traditional female field but she could have been at the top of any company or industry. I believed I could be successful in any number of industries because of my personal qualities. I thought that most degrees did not prepare one for a profession, so I choose a degree simply because I loved the subject matter.

I graduated with a degree in psychology, and hoped that the insight into the way people act would serve me well in any job. As a student I conducted surveys for a market research company and continued with the company after I graduated. I learned to use a mainframe computer to produce research reports and realized that computers were really all about logic. Now logic I can handle! Programming gave me a trade with which I could support myself. Having computer skills was a true blessing for which I was thankful. I could make as much as a tradesman with my brain instead of my back. I was able to purchase a little frame house that had ten foot ceilings and linoleum throughout (snazzy). My landlord used the money to buy a new car and I was very proud of having my own place.

Eventually I had to decide between technology or business management. During those years computer time was always at a premium. I worked late and I was up all hours of the night because the computer performed most efficiently with fewer users. Those long hours helped me decide business was best for me. I also saw that any perks available went to the account executives in sales. In retrospect I think I made the right decision. I did enjoy solving the puzzles that came with programming and I am extremely thankful that I do not fear technology that is such a part of modern daily life.

I was hired for a market research project manager position in California. My house rented quickly and I made the move back to Los Angeles. I began to understand what a logical transition it had been from psychology to market research. The management team at the LA firm all had psychology degrees too. My new office was in Century City, a development adjacent to Beverly Hills. It had office towers, condominiums, and an open air mall. Despite the great surroundings, I didn't like the company and quit after one year.

I wanted to go into real estate. I was ready for something that didn't have me glued to a desk and a computer day and night. I thought I could start by re-doing old houses. I loved working on projects of all kinds and felt like it would be a creative outlet, but the costs to get into a property were just too high in California. Even then, a house I looked at for $200,000 literally fell down before it could be sold. It was time to go east!

Real Estate Here I Come

I came back to Texas, sold my house and went to Europe for three months. When I returned I moved into a "fixer-upper" and earned my real estate license while I did freelance computer work. I sold a few houses and over a period of time bought three more modest frame houses to refurbish and rent. Renovation and rentals were fine but selling residential property was not for me. I did lots of cleaning and painting and learned to tape and bed walls (don't let me work on your home). At one point I was even mowing lawns on three houses every week. I loved the variety each day but needed more of a long-term plan.

I had seen my mom go through life as a person who loved her work, but didn't like or understand finance. Financial decisions were nerve wracking for her. I realized finance was what made things happen. Don't get me wrong, I was intimidated by math and unsophisticated about business, but I really needed to understand this stuff! After taking some lower level math classes I was admitted to the prestigious MBA program at Southern Methodist University (SMU).

Admission to the program was just the beginning. Almost all of the other students walked in with business degrees, and to be honest, I earned "Fs" on my first tests. It was *ugly*, but there was too much money involved to even consider failure. I cried... and studied and studied and studied.

Sometimes pure determination will carry you even if the subject is not a natural match for your talents. It was hard to find a tutor in graduate school, so I had to beg a professor to give me extra help. Getting his buy-in required a lengthy conversation because he thought he would be wasting his time on me. He believed I would just take my degree, get married, and not use it. I had to demonstrate that I was worth his time, was actually smart enough to learn the subject matter, and intended to have a career. In the end, he helped me. I have to assume that those kinds of conversations with female students don't still occur, but they might. By the way, my MBA class was fifty-fifty male and female. Completing my Masters degree was the most difficult goal I had ever set out to complete. Midway through my coursework the testing center results indicated I was so unsuited to the graduate business program that the advisor was amazed I had even tried to achieve it.

Fortunately, I have other strengths in business, and I am extremely persistent. Classwork became much more interesting to me as we proceeded deeper into the subject of real estate. I am now comfortable in situations where people casually throw around rates of return and general investment scenarios. Throughout my career my degree has consistently added to my credibility with employers. In particular, it opened the door for my first job in commercial real estate.

My first real estate position was with a developer. I was told that the company income came from leasing and no matter how well you performed through the years, you would not move into a VP position without having spent some time in the leasing department. My prospective boss thought it would be better for me to do leasing first. I thought leasing (sales) could not be any worse than school. Wow, what a fortunate move for me. I loved it.

Buildings are so "real" and the changes made are easily seen. Office and industrial buildings perform a duty, but a shopping center has so much character and always the possibility of fun. There are simple or great meals and treasures to be found. Many home design or apparel stores show off such creativity and the talents of many designers. It is always a challenge to take a project—low, middle, or luxury to the next level of success. Even today it is like working a puzzle where I (as part of a team) get to change the pieces.

I was fortunate to start in the business with talented professionals who could visualize, layout, and create a center from dirt. We built centers throughout the Dallas area. My job was to work with all the "small shop" stores. During this period

I met and married my husband and after a few years we had a little boy.

Shortly thereafter, in the late eighties, a profound downturn hit the area. Texas was overbuilt and red-lined. No lenders would take a risk on a property in Texas, and any investors or developers who held assets in land or buildings saw their wealth evaporate. This was my first experience with the cyclical nature of real estate. I was laid off and really experienced panic. A long-time friend calmed me down, and helped me make a list of how to survive the layoff and how to approach a job search.

Traveling Mom

My former office location in Century City played a part in my next career move. I joined a large company that invested pension fund money in real estate nationally. This is considered an "institutional" investor. The properties must be of a quality and in a location such that retirement funds would be safe, and yet have the opportunity to increase in value. My prospective employer wanted me to lease Century City Mall in LA. I knew that center like the back of my charge card.

I had walked over there for lunch every day for a year in my prior life, long before I had an inkling that I was ever going to go into real estate. My problem was that the property was in Los Angeles and I lived in Dallas with my husband and baby. *"No problem"* the company said, just choose which three days a week you want to be in LA. We fly you there. What? My husband's work did not require him to travel and there were no local real estate jobs in Dallas, so together we decided to work it out. Century City was a great property and my new employer was a great company. I suddenly went from leasing a large discount center in Mesquite TX to leasing a high profile property bordering Beverly Hills.

The Los Angeles location made leasing a very interesting endeavor. After working on the project for a while my friend and I began to collect store names . . . things like "Wanna Buy a Watch" (on Melrose in LA), "Dam and Dam Naughty" (also on Melrose—owned by a lovely Vietnamese couple named Dam that I later leased a space to), "Chris and Dick's World of Paneling" (in Salt Lake City when we were lost), and "Ole's Truly Kosher Mexican Café" (near the studios in LA; it's gone now but has evidently been replaced by "Mexikosher").

Those years—traveling every week—were wild for me personally. I usually left Tuesday morning and came back late Thursday evening. For the first few years I was gone for two nights, three weeks out of every month. We hired a live-in nanny. She spoke only a small amount of English.

We took her to visit friends, to her church, and to English classes to be sure she was happy. We decided to move to a bigger home so we could again have a guest room. On moving day she announced she had a new job with a well-to-do family that had a housekeeper, a cook, and a babysitter. She thought her sister would come and babysit our son, and her plan was that the two sisters would live together in our home. Whoa Nelly! Not so fast. When we began working with nannies, we had hoped we would be able to say *"Oh—she has been with us forever,"* but sadly we ended up with a different nanny every year or two.

I recall the time my missing make-up brush was found in the kitchen next to the pastry brush. That was courtesy of a very sweet former girl scout from Guatemala, who casually carried the groceries on her head. I took her to the park with my son and she was so surprised when she slid down the slide and her skirt went over her head.

One time we hired a middle-aged lady who had been taking care of elderly people. She said she wanted to work with younger people in a more cheerful setting. She moved in and I let her bring her cat, which was a major concession on my part as we were not cat people. My main condition was that we be honest with each other if things weren't working out. We needed some notice if she wanted to leave. Things went smoothly for several months. One Friday, she warned us her sister was coming early the next morning to pick her up for a weekend trip, and not to worry if we heard them up and around. When I woke up, I found the three-page note of apology. She had been offered a job caring for an elderly person for more pay, but the offer was only good if she could start immediately. She had actually moved everything out, but left her color TV (too heavy) and . . . her cat.

A trusted caregiver is the lifeblood of a traveling mom or any working mom. There I was, standing in my gown on that Saturday morning with my life upside down. I thought I had to have a sitter who had worked for someone I knew, or for a friend of a friend. After a few years, I worked up the nerve to advertise in the paper (now an outdated method I guess) and actually found some wonderful people that way. That is a tip for you moms out there.

I developed a special bond with other traveling mothers in our business. One tenant rep had children a little older than mine and called me to let me know her high-school age "straight A" son had come home with green hair—look for it to happen in a couple of years, she warned. She also let me know when her daughter—active in the Young Republicans Club, came home from college with a tongue pierce. Fortunately, both have turned into great adults.

A broker in LA shared that she didn't think she could handle more kids because she couldn't handle any more nannies. Her nanny started on a cleaning binge and decided to clean up the fingerprints around the light switches by getting the paint from the garage and painting over that area in each room—yes, each room of her house.

I made every effort to be with and enjoy my son, and was involved with his school, sports, and scouting events. He has grown up to be a wonderful young man. I am fortunate my marriage did not suffer, but don't take a traveling position like this lightly. It is very difficult.

Retail Real Estate Leasing and Networking

I have a good reputation and I am proud of it. I am not a genius; I just work hard and always remain polite. This approach has served me well and I believe it would serve anyone well. The development and leasing of shopping centers industry is national and even international. It is big business. Despite the size of the field, we often work with the same person many times over a career. At Century City we changed the mix of merchandise offered in the center by taking it higher end. This strategy was successful and the center sales picked up. That was many years ago, but due to the interconnected nature of the industry, I have been able to maintain contact with many of the same tenant representatives I worked with then. I renewed a lease with an individual at Zales for a store in Plano TX. Later I completed a new deal with him to bring a Disney store to Century City, and then worked with him to put an Ann Taylor store in another mall in LA. I even leased him some office space in Dallas in the process.

Granted, we both have had long careers but our paths continue to cross. Each time I was working for a different landlord and he was working on behalf of a different tenant. If you are honest, responsive, and polite, the door for more business is always open.

I feel enriched by the individuals I have gotten to know. Yes there are a few thorns, but by far the people in our business are great folks and we have a broad shared experience. I think everyone in my industry feels the same. We work hard, pull out our hair over tricky issues or knuckleheads, and later get together over lunch or dinner. The diversity of people, businesses, and locations make retail interesting enough that I can continue in the same profession or even the same position for many years. It is never boring. So far I have worked on projects in TX, CA, WA, OR, NV, AL, GA, MN, and AZ.

When working with prospective tenants (or any client), I have learned to ask them about their history, and what they did before becoming a shoe store owner or pizza franchisee. The level of talent, education, and passion a "ma and pa" tenant may bring to the table can be amazing. I have met some tenants who were very interesting well-traveled individuals, some very unsophisticated but earnest people, and some irrational characters. The most informative question I ever ask a prospective tenant is *"What differentiates you from your competitors?"* This elicits more detail and insight than you might imagine and applies to local and national tenants alike.

A couple of years ago, a well-respected national tenant representative shared some advice with me. I found it very interesting and it still rings true. She said that a tenant who knows they need a location in the "A" rated center will focus a good amount of time making sure it happens. However, it is different when they are considering the "B" and "C" rated locations. In this scenario, the landlord's rep or broker can make a big difference because the quality of the centers may not be that different. The transaction often goes to the rep or broker who follows up, sends accurate, useful information, and makes a true effort to complete a transaction.

Early on I was working for a warehouse "expert." If I asked a shopping center question he would never say *"I don't know."* He would make up an answer, putting me in an even worse position. That's when I started networking with other women in my industry. I learned to do research, and then present the choices to my boss. My life improved considerably. You show up with solutions (which is what they really want anyway). I actively searched for other women in retail leasing who could help me. We have now been friends for years and years. I have also become much more comfortable asking questions and brainstorming with the guys. I have worked with some great ones. If you don't have a network of friends in your industry, start finding them. It makes a difference.

Meeting in groups is not a substitute for one-on-one conversations. Many issues do not come out in a group setting. In a one-on-one conversation, individuals are much more open about what motivates them, what challenges they are facing, and what their outside interests are.

People fascinate me. I love to meet with them. I also find it is easy to call upon them with an idea or a question about a specific business issue after I get to know them. This is true for colleagues or clients in the industry, or even competitors. Recognize that no tenant or client will take a deal simply based on friendship, but I find the people I know might give my transactions more immediate attention, or at least they may remove the roadblocks.

Everyone in real estate has experienced significant change since the recession that started in 2008. Many of my friends and contacts now work for different companies. The downturn changed the economy. The real estate landscape will never return to business as usual.

Borrowing by small businesses is still difficult, which slows the pace of small shop leasing. Limited capital requires that each new deal is considered from every angle before approval, and each transaction takes longer. The downturn is passing, but none of us will forget the trauma of a lock-up in business that took place so recently. Real estate is cyclical, sometimes drastically so, but I am fortunate to have found a career that is most often fun and creative. I am proud when I complete a deal and shepherd an idea to fruition. I enjoy the people I work with and I continue to learn a tremendous amount by dealing with tenants in all types of businesses. There is little repetition and every week is fresh and different. The "business" is good!

About Linda Alexander

Linda Alexander has a proven track record leasing shopping centers, primarily in Texas and California. She has worked with developers and pension fund advisors to create value in malls, lifestyle, and power centers, and has completed leasing transactions with an array of national restaurant and retail tenants.

Linda grew up in Los Angeles, resides in Texas, and holds an MBA from Southern Methodist University in Dallas, and a Texas Brokers License.

Email: Linda.alex@verizon.net

Chapter 2

Pause for Life
by Lynn Dowdle

There has always been a "knowingness" that has prevailed over any adversity that has come my way in life. There have been hours, maybe even days or weeks where I paused between confidence and doubt as to what direction to take. Regardless of the length of that gap, I always got to a point where I knew everything was going to be—not just okay—but everything would be better . . . after the pause.

I was a junior at the University of Texas and lived in a small apartment complex in a very beautiful and private section of Austin, Texas. One day I was casually approached by a neighbor. She began to lament about the fact that she was graduating and she did not want to give up her business. Throughout her years at the university, she had established quite a successful bakery business, and in fact, she was commissioned by most of the thriving restaurants in Austin, to bake cheesecakes which were to be served in each establishment. As she went on, she leaned in, looked at me, and with sad eyes asked sincerely, "*Do you know anyone who bakes cheesecakes?*". . . pause . . . I boldly proclaimed, "*Why yes! I bake cheesecakes!*" She broke into an enthusiastic "*Perfect! Then you can have my business! I will give you a list of the restaurants. You contact them and just have fun! You'll love it!*" We shook hands and hugged and parted ways—each of us with a brand new outlook on the future. That was all fine and well, but I had never made a cheesecake in my life! Panic time! So like every resourceful woman would do, I called one of the most famous bakeries in town. *"I know this may sound like an unusual question"* I said, *"but could I get your cheesecake recipe?"* The voice on the other end didn't miss a beat. *"Why sure—here you go—I happen to know it by heart."* He was the head baker and within what seemed like two seconds, I had found the buried treasure! The recipe would save me! For two years, I made up to fifty cheesecakes at a time for the still thriving restaurants. I learned to buy in bulk and I was given access to the industrial type kitchen in a restaurant where I had worked previously as a cocktail waitress.

This one opportunity—foreshadowed by a pause—allowed me to ask myself, *"What are you yearning for? What will make your heart sing?"* For me it was certainly a surprise— answering the way I did—but I knew deep down inside of me that my response came from the bottom of my heart. It allowed me to stretch into something I had never done before—to live dangerously, "faking it 'til I made it." It brought passion and excitement to me—it woke me up! All I had to do was say *"Yes"* to the possibility. It was scary and fantastic all at the same time. I would do it again in a second. I remind myself that the freedom to choose came from the pause. It allowed me to dig deep and find my truth before I knew it was my truth.

Later in my life, a friend of mine encouraged me to get into the commercial real estate business. After some—okay—a lot of resistance, I finally agreed. She then found me my first job where I would stay for five years, learning the business of leasing retail strip centers for a third party. I was given a desk and a chair and a phone. One of the female senior brokers in the office was to mentor me. That was great with me, but my mentor wasn't too keen on taking time out of her day to teach me—the newbie. After about a month, my mentor, somewhat frustrated, pulled me into her office. She closed the door and for what seemed an eternity, told me I would never make it in the business; I didn't have the brains it took and I was basically incompetent . . . and on and on and on. Finally, at the end of her rant, she looked at me and asked "*Do you have anything to say?*" I paused, took a deep breath, and calmly replied, "*Thank you.*" "*Thank you?*" she asked. "What do you mean, thank you?" I looked across her big desk and straight into her eyes, and after a pause I said, "*Ever since I was a little girl, whenever anyone said I couldn't do something, I always did it. So thank you.*" I smiled and politely got up from my chair and walked out of her office. She left to go to another company. I wouldn't have listened to her again anyway.

After five years at that original company, I began a new gig. I was given a desk, but this time it was in a fancy office which was on the 37th floor, with my very own window overlooking the sky line of Dallas. This time I knew what I was doing and where I was headed! And the best part? Guess whose desk I got? My mentor's! The one who told me I didn't have a chance. Today, I have been in real estate for twenty-three years. Three years ago, I started my own company and I have never looked back. At the time it felt like I was literally jumping off of a cliff. Now it seems like this is where I am meant to be. I know I am competent and I have what it takes because I got here— regardless of what one person said many years ago.

I am often reminded that many successful people have been visited by naysayers at the beginning of their journey. Just recently, I heard of an author who was told that her one and only chapter was never going to go anywhere. She knew intuitively that she was born to write. Not too long ago, her book was on the New York Best Sellers list for over two years!

Once again, I look back to the pause. This time the pause was for digging deep within myself to find my truth, to fight for my authentic self, and leave one person's opinion as just that—her opinion. I was able to pause to go to my center. At that moment, I knew I had a voice and I was fixin' to use it, as we say here in Texas! It was a small bravery in hindsight, but the opportunity to stand up for who I was helped lay the foundation for more of that in my life. What I know now is my life is full of small daily braveries.

My dear niece, whose soul resides in heaven, used to always remind me, *"Do something every day that scares you."* I smile as I know there is honest truth in that—it's what unleashes our power. I try to keep everything in perspective, knowing that it's not brave unless we're scared.

There is a lot to be said about a pause. It allows us to breathe and to stay calm. It allows us to respond rather than react. There have been plenty of times in my life that I have reacted without pause, don't get me wrong, but I know for sure that when I take time to pause, I always win. I win the opportunity to set my intention, to have the courage to ask myself the hard question, and to authentically claim the answer. Our lives are a series of events that we can learn from. I figure it's a lot easier to be intentional and try and move forward, than to set myself up for failure by not listening to the depth of who I am.

Bar none, the best contribution I have made to this world is my two beautiful incredible adult children. I'm sure I have many more accomplishments ahead of me, but none will parallel the opportunity that I have had by raising my two best friends in the world. I was a single mother for many years and during those years, there were plenty of opportunities for growth, shall we say. I was often the mother and the father and many times life's challenges hit me dead on. Often during those years, I would awaken early in the morning just to create a "time to breathe," a time to reflect, a time to get centered, and a time to find the truth in how I was living my life as a woman and as a mother. I can honestly say that those mornings—of great pause—were what kept me going. Before the busyness of the day, I was able to pause for what I knew to be the organic, grassroots answers from God—the real stuff. I look back on those times and I know I was being lead. I was being guided with His grace—something I could never have done for myself.

I'm grateful for the long pauses as well as the short ones. I'm grateful for the moments where I listened to something greater than myself, and in return I was provided with absolutely everything I needed. Not wanted . . . I said needed.

When my son turned eighteen and went off to college, I had an amazing experience. One night, in the middle of my sleep, I sat straight up in bed. Knowing that my son was for all practical purposes, grown and gone, I was in a panic and a question hit me like a ton of bricks. *"Did you give him everything he will need to be a productive, amazing man in this life? Did you do the very best you knew how—because guess what? Your time is up!"* I took a deep breath and I paused, and in an instant I knew the answer was *"Yes."* I felt confident now, and that confidence was rooted in my longtime practice of the daily morning pause; all of those years—pausing to listen the best I knew how, digging deep to hear the answers to my own questions, hearing God, my authentic self through my intuition (which is God-given), and shutting out the voices of the world just like I had done when I heard the critical comments from my once "mentor."

There is often a spot of time offered us—sometimes short and sometimes longer. We must take that time. We must ask the questions, *"What am I yearning for?" "What do I need more of to lead a life of excellence, yet still be vulnerable in this world, living open-hearted and opening up to possibility?"*

No matter how scary it is, we must have the courage to say it all, to use our voice, and to set our intention for a life well lived. When it's the very hardest and we have lost our way, let's just pause—a little longer, or again—and breathe, and our life becomes our own. Let's welcome the pauses. Let's escort them in. After all, life is what happens between the pauses. I hope you find the miracle in that.

About Lynn Dowdle

Lynn Dowdle is a highly recognized, top producing real estate broker with extensive experience in the Lone Star State of Texas. She founded Dowdle Real Estate in 2011 after a long career with several major corporations such as Trammell Crow and Staubach.

Named as a Heavy Hitter for the past fifteen years, her comprehensive background and relationships enhance and strengthen her ability to serve clients throughout Texas.

Besides her professional accomplishments, Lynn is a founder of an organization aligned with World Vision, "If You Knew," raising over two million dollars for clean water in Africa (IfYouKnew.org). She is an active volunteer as a budget counselor with New Friends New Life, an organization which restores and empowers formerly trafficked girls and sexually exploited women and their children.

In her free time, she enjoys all outdoor sports. Her greatest accomplishment to date? Her daughter and son who she coins "her best friends in life."

Email: Lynn@DowdleRealEstate.com
LinkedIn: LinkedIn.com/pub/lynn-dowdle/12/720/397

Chapter 3

Working in Russia:
Stepping Out of Your Comfort Zone
by Brenda Ford

If you are considering working abroad, whether it be a long-term career or a short-term assignment, be prepared to "discover yourself" in ways you never thought possible.

The most important lessons I learned while working in Moscow were not the business aspects of the retail market or commercial real estate development trends in Eastern Europe. The greatest lesson was what I learned about myself—attitude, flexibility, perception, and inner strength.

Russia has played a very important role in teaching me critical life lessons, first when I was a teenager and then again later in my commercial real estate career. What I want to share with you is not about specific real estate trends at the time I was working in Moscow; nor about lessons on calculating square meters versus square footage in lease negotiations, but about what it takes mentally, physically, and emotionally to prosper and succeed in a country that is so different from America. I want to share about stepping out of your comfort zone and taking on a great adventure!

At age seventeen, I moved out of my parent's house and was completely independent, armed with only a high-school degree, and working a job waiting tables. One day I walked into a Church's Fried Chicken, and while waiting on my order, I noticed a box that read, *"Win a trip to the country that wins the world chess tournament."* On a whim, I filled out the contest form and dropped it in the box. To my great surprise, the Soviet Union won the world chess tournament and my name was drawn to win the trip! So at age eighteen, I found myself on a plane to what was then the communist U.S.S.R. (before the fall of the Iron Curtain). Little did I know I would be back one day as a working professional woman in a commercial real estate career during one of the biggest real estate booms across Russia.

That two-week trip marked a turning point in my life. On the way home, I made clear and conscious decisions just hours before my plane landed back on U.S. soil; that I would set higher goals for myself and move forward in changing my life, and choose to follow a road that could potentially give me a professional "career" versus simply a "job." Step number one was to further my education. While continuing to work full time, I enrolled part-time in college, taking classes until I completed my degree.

During the course of my transition from waitress to part-time college student, I landed a job at a commercial real estate company as a secretary. As I gained more knowledge and was promoted along the way, I knew that retail commercial real estate was the industry around which I wanted to build my career. After receiving my college diploma, I was hired by a real estate company to handle the leasing of two malls, and to assist in pitching new business development. My career in the United States was beginning to take off, and would continue to grow in areas of lease negotiations on behalf of landlords; preparing SWOT analysis for various regional enclosed malls and creating merchandise plans and budgets for client investors.

More than thirty years after returning from the most important trip of my life (compliments of Church's Fried Chicken), I came across an opportunity for an available position at a large real estate company in Moscow. It was for a three-year assignment as a consultant for several Russian commercial real estate developers who were building mega malls in a country that by now was stumbling a bit on its way to "westernization." They were looking for someone with "western" experience who could bring over best practices regarding lease negotiations between landlords and tenants; merchandising plan preparation; SWOT analysis; and best and highest use analysis. Shopping mall development was rampant because there was a severe lack of square footage for modern retailers entering Eastern Europe. At the time, it was like the California Gold Rush of 1849, except instead of eastern fortune-seekers rushing west with their mining tools, their entire belongings, and dollar signs in their eyes, it was western retailers rushing east with dreams of success, stacks of leasing documents, and sales volumes in their eyes. Some of the U.S. retailers entering the market were Starbucks, Nike, Subway, and Payless Shoes.

At the time, I was close to turning fifty, married, and with a son in college. I was also thirsty for a new challenge, seriously questioning if yet another adventure might be waiting for me. After discussion with my family, I applied for the three-year assignment in Moscow, and four weeks after my 50th birthday, I landed at Moscow's Sheremetyevo International Airport with two very large suitcases, my work visa, and a smile from ear to ear.

Upon arriving at the airport, I thought perhaps a translator from my new company might be there to help me with the language barrier (although I did take a short Russian-language introductory course, I did not speak any Russian) or that a personal driver might be waiting for me, holding a sign that said *"Welcome to Moscow, Ms. Ford."* These were reasonable assumptions because, in preparing for my move, I had spoken to several expats from Coca-Cola, Toyota, and Frito-Lay, and they all had a Russian "buddy" (one who also spoke English) assigned to help assist them in their new environment. However, that was not to be the case for me. I walked out of customs and into a sea of people shoulder-to-shoulder, yelling and rushing around with carts overloaded with large brown cardboard boxes, wrapped and tied up with yards of string, worn suitcases with what looked like Saran wrap around them, and big nylon net plaid shopping bags filled to capacity. I stood in the middle of this mayhem, searching for some clue of what I should do next. My next three years living and working in Russia unfolded in similar, often chaotic fashion.

Working in Russia definitely had many challenges, not the least of which was the language barrier. Not having a grasp of the language, I was always at the mercy of various translators (some much better than others) when I attended business meetings or when I was involved in any type of negotiations. One day, I was meeting with a very rich and influential Russian developer who had just returned from Dubai. (Dubai's economy at that time resembled Russia's, with an incredible amount of money being invested in shopping malls—but Dubai was more like Russia on steroids.) Toward the end of our fairly pleasant conversation, my potential client mentioned some of the unbelievably high rents his colleague was getting in Dubai. My casual response was, *"Wow, you have got to be kidding me."* (Did I mention some translators were better than others?) Translated to him as, *"You dirty rotten liar! There is no way that can be true!"* And that's when the trouble really began. He clamped his mouth shut, glared at me across the table with his nostrils flaring in and out like a raging bull, and pounded his fists on the table. He then abruptly pushed his chair back, slamming it against the wall, and stormed out of the room while yelling loudly at both me and the translator. No worries, though, no one came in and drug me off to a place in Siberia where I lived out the rest of my life in chains and shackles. I tried to salvage that new business pitch later on; however, that real estate deal was won by my company's strongest competitor. Because I was directly involved in not gaining that particular client's business, I learned a very valuable (and expensive) lesson. When working outside the United States, whether you are in commercial real estate or selling any other type of service to a potential client, never should you use colloquialisms or "sayings" or any type of slang when pitching new business.

Learning Russian customs was also a challenge because these customs (and/or superstitions) are much different than those in the U.S. For example, in Russia one does not shake hands over the threshold of an office entrance, one must be careful to select flower colors appropriate to the occasion, and one does not exchange money after sundown. A custom that especially and totally amazed me was that no one leaves the dinner table while there is unfinished wine or an open bottle of vodka still on the table. It was sort of like when your mom used to say, *"Now clean your plate, dear, before you excuse yourself from the dinner table."* However, in this case we are talking booze, not mashed potatoes and green beans!

My first Russian business dinner was at a nice restaurant with eight of us (six Russian men, Svetlana who was our marketing director, and me—a girl from Texas used to drinking iced tea with dinner) celebrating the "win" of a big assignment. "Celebrating" is the key word here. Along with a fabulous feast of amazing food, the host also ordered several bottles of vodka and wine. (Recall that there were only eight of us, and the custom is to leave no liquor behind.) After about three hours of eating and polishing off a full bottle of vodka and four bottles of wine, we still had one opened and almost full bottle of vodka and a half-bottle of opened wine on the table.

So commenced an additional three hours of toasts and cheers and clinking of glasses. *"Salud!"* Clink clink . . . *"to the best team in Moscow! To our new client! Salud!"* As we slowly made our way through the rest of the wine and vodka, glasses continued to be raised, and speech became increasingly slurred. Someone blurted out, *"To Svet, Svet, to Svetlana for. . . ahh . . . for her . . . let's see now . . . Yeah, for her support in making us . . . I mean, I mean . . . in getting us the support in presentation materials!"* Clink clink. Svetlana hiccupped, raised her glass, and managed with some difficulty to yell out *"And to Brenda, to Brenda, for not calling our new client a liar!"* . . . Clink clink.

At one point in that evening, the host stood up at the head of the table, sat back down and then stood back up. He held onto the table with one hand, while with the other he held a full glass of vodka, waving it in front of him like it was a magic wand and sloshing vodka over the rim as he attempted to make the final toast of the evening. He sounded as though he had just filled his mouth with marbles—no one understood that last toast, which I think was something about how he loved everyone at the table, and he also loved everyone in the restaurant and would love them forever and ever. Yes, this is how many of our dinners ended. My best advice when attending "business dinners" in Russia (or any other country for that matter), is that you fully understand the local customs and prepare yourself ahead of time in order not to over-indulge, or risk the chance of insulting the host.

A third major challenge was getting used to a different workplace culture. (By "culture," I mean the type of thinking, certain working styles, and methods of communicating—basically, the way of doing things.) One can conduct research, talk to other knowledgeable people, and read all kinds of articles about the culture of a country, but that is like reading about and asking how to ride a bicycle. Until you actually get on a bicycle (without training wheels) and experience the ride, you really have no idea about the coordination or balance it takes, nor do you anticipate the inevitable bumps and bruises.

I was absolutely shocked by the Russian workplace culture. Probably the biggest and most challenging part of that culture was how companies managed their employees—they verbally abused them, or at least that was my initial perception. In America, we are not accustomed to our bosses running out of their offices to our desks, waving papers back and forth above their heads, all the while angrily screaming at the top of their lungs about something we did or did not do correctly. Can you imagine working in that kind of environment? I was horrified; however, in our Moscow office, everyone took this behavior with a grain of salt. No one ever retaliated or cried or got upset in the least—not once. The first time I witnessed this behavior in my department was when Anna, who sat next to me, was the target. I couldn't figure out what she had done (or not done) because all the yelling from our boss was in Russian, but it did not take a rocket scientist to figure out that he was mad—no, he was livid! Anna didn't flinch or get teary-eyed or start shaking. On the contrary, she acted as if he had screamed, *"Hooray, Hooray--Anna just got a promotion!"*

One of the most wonderful things about growing older is that you gain a much better understanding of what works for you and what absolutely does not. Being screamed at by a boss, even once, was not going to work for me. I knew immediately and without a doubt that I would not tolerate it—in fact, I was the one who got all shaky and embarrassed and humiliated when Anna was the one in trouble, not me. So I immediately walked into Mr. Boss' office, closed the door, and very slowly, in a soft, calm voice, said *"Hey, listen. I have heard employees in other departments being yelled at, and now I have seen you do the same to Anna. I want you to know that if you ever have an issue with me, instead of marching out to my desk and throwing a temper tantrum in front of the entire office, I request that you instead call me into your office and talk to me in a civilized manner."* He looked at me, squinted and said in a very stern voice with a thick Russian accent, *"What you mean temper tantrum? I don't throw nothing at nobody."* After explaining what "throwing a temper tantrum" meant, I acknowledged that I was working in a Russian office, was aware of the many cultural differences between Russian and American workplaces, and was willing to accept most of them. However, I asked that he honor my request on this one, and I can proudly say he did. We ended up having a great working relationship, closing more retail development business than any other company in Moscow during that time. And you know what that meant? Yes, more dinners celebrating the wins!

If your career happens to land you in an office in one of the Eastern European countries, be accepting of the radically different workplace environment, but do draw the line where it absolutely does not work for you. Communicating in a way that empowers both you and the person you are talking to is extremely rewarding, and you will realize how it strengthens the business relationship between the two of you.

An unexpected and wonderful experience in my three years living and working in Russia was the opportunity to meet and mentor Akmaral, a young woman from Kazakhstan who had graduated from college a year earlier and was new to the commercial real estate profession. She was struggling with her decision as to whether or not to return to school for her graduate degree. After many evenings of conversations, emotional breakdowns, and also tons of laughter, Akmaral eventually pushed through her fear of failing, her fear of the unknown, and her fear of such a serious commitment, and went on to earn her MBA from Harvard University. We remain in close touch today, and I consider our relationship one of the greatest blessings of my entire Russian adventure. I mention this because whether your career is here in the U.S. or abroad in a foreign country, one of the most rewarding feelings is to know you have made a small difference in someone else's life, and a friendship forever.

Today I am happy and pleased that I had the opportunity to work with a team of young Russian men and women on the leasing and merchandising of one of the largest malls ever built in Russia; and that I consulted with several oligarchs and various banks on highest and best use for their land; and that I implemented training programs for young professionals entering the retail market that are still in place today. But by far my greatest lesson was learning about myself and who I am as a professional fifty-plus year old working in this awesome industry of retail commercial real estate—breaking through what I thought were my limits; tackling an adventure to create a fun journey in life; and communicating in a way that is powerful and rewarding.

These stories represent only a tiny sample of the trials and tribulations I experienced while working in Russia; I have many, many more stories. You would be amazed at the countless incidents—some good and some not so good—caused by the language barrier, the unusual customs and superstitions, and the difference in cultures. Working in a foreign country absolutely takes courage, flexibility, and a great attitude. Nonetheless, I strongly recommend that you do your best to find work abroad at some point in your career, no matter your age. You may end up inadvertently insulting someone every now and then, or you may crawl out of a restaurant on your hands and knees after a "celebratory" dinner. Yet you may also discover some inner strength that you never knew you had—for example, the strength to stand up for yourself without creating conflict—because you have learned to *communicate* in a way you never dreamed possible. You may discover that fear stops you from growing and stepping out into some risky areas—because you have learned to *break through* some of your perceived barriers. You may discover a friendship for life—because you stopped and took the time to mentor a younger person.

Paka (pronounced "pauk-ah," which is "goodbye" in Russian and is also the extent of my Russian vocabulary). If I knew anymore Russian, I would say to you, *"If you have any desire to work outside the United States, go for it. It is never too late!"*

Lessons Learned and Career Tips

- To really grow as a person and in your career, be willing to step out of your comfort zone. Not only welcome new challenges, but actively seek them out.

- No matter the stage of your career or your age, it's never too late to entertain and say *"Yes!"* to new and different adventures.

- Testing the limits and breaking through.

- New adventures often bring unexpected and delightful blessings.

- Remain flexible and open to new ideas and career paths.

- Keep your sense of humor and a good attitude, which will stand you in good stead.

About Brenda Ford

During her tenure in Russia, Brenda Ford was the first woman in history in the Moscow office to be promoted from Associate Director to National Director. Currently, she is Vice President and Leasing Specialist for a global commercial real estate company where she is responsible for the overall development and execution of leasing strategies for U.S. retail projects throughout the Southwest.

LinkedIn: LinkedIn.com/in/brendaford1

Chapter 4

How to Develop
Single Tenant Leased Properties
by Pamela J. Goodwin

"The secret of getting ahead is getting started."
-Mark Twain

Growing up I always wanted to be a hotel interior designer. This desire grew out of my fascination with a beautiful hotel we visited on a summer vacation to Florida. We didn't stay in that hotel. We stayed in a nearby motel. I also wanted to be a famous Hollywood actress and a successful woman business owner. So many things to be, so little time. After graduating from the University of Nebraska-Lincoln with a degree in Interior Design, I was offered a position designing hotel interiors with J.W. Marriott at their corporate headquarters in Bethesda, MD. I thought it would be my dream job, but decided not to leave my family and relocate. Instead, I stayed in my home town of Omaha, NE and took an in-house interior designer position with a large office and shopping center developer with an annual salary of $17,000. Unfortunately, I was not designing grandiose hotel lobbies, but rather I was designing law, real estate, and call center offices, and learning a lot. It was when this company decided to create one of the first Power Retail Centers in Cottonwood, Arizona that I was officially hooked on development. I am a very visual person, and I found it fascinating to be involved in a project where vacant property is transformed into a retail center. My love for retail and restaurant real estate continued to grow.

Now, looking back, it seems totally natural that I would be drawn to retail real estate. My father owned his own poultry business and sold his chickens to all of the local restaurants in Omaha. My mother loved to take us kids shopping, especially for clothes—and I loved going to the big shopping malls. The design, bright lights, and all of the colors are what made the big shopping mall special to me. I loved eating out and I loved shopping, so even though I didn't realize it until after college, a career in retail development was a perfect fit for me.

Each job I took, I wanted to make sure I learned something that would further my development expertise. Over that course of several years I worked for a few large shopping center developers on the landlord side of commercial real estate, but I wanted to learn more about the tenant side. When I was offered a position with Brinker International, Inc., one of the world's leading casual dining restaurant companies with more than 1,500 restaurants, I jumped at the opportunity. Whether rich or poor, people need to eat. I was hired as a Property Development Manager to oversee new Chili's development in four states, and then later promoted to oversee On the Border throughout the country. The property development role is between the real estate manager and construction department. In less than three years, I developed more than fifty free standing restaurants from the ground up and was also crowned the "Pepper Queen" for fighting City of Dallas and winning the approval to allow the large Chili's 3D iconic red chili pepper to be placed at the entrance of each restaurant.

A big part of my development job at Brinker involved working with land owners who leased their property to Brinker to put in a Chili's, for example. These lessors would then sell the Chili's ground lease to investors and make a big profit on each property. I thought to myself, if they can do it, I can do it! The push I needed to pursue this type of business was hearing a song by a musical group called Sugarland. The song, "*Something More*," motivated me to leave my "secure" corporate job and start my own firm. The year was 2006. It was the best business decision I have ever made and I'm glad I had the courage to stop making other people money and look out for myself. I knew I needed an experienced partner to help me get started. I approached a few of the landlords who were currently developing property and asked if they would help me get started in my own business. I found a partner within a few months, and Goodwin Commercial Properties was created. The focus would be on acquiring one to five acre parcels and developing single tenant pad sites for national restaurant and non-restaurant retailers.

Starting your own business can be very exciting and scary at the same time, but also very rewarding. I wanted to create my own path of success—on my timeline. It was the first time I ever looked forward to going to work on Monday mornings.

Characteristics of Women Business Owners

- Women business owners are prepared to face risk: most (sixty-six percent) are willing to take above average or substantial risks for business investments.

- Women and men business owners have different management styles. Women emphasize relationship building, as well as fact gathering, and are more likely to consult with experts and employees.

I have always enjoyed the thrill of the hunt—finding an opportunity no one else may see and going after it. How many times have you driven by a location and your gut tells you that would be a perfect location for a Starbucks, a Walgreens, or a Chase bank—and then several months later, it opens on the exact location, as you predicted? I have always had an instinct about site selection. Part of my instinct is knowing when a current use is outdated and what retail concept would excel at that same location. How exciting!

An Introduction to Developing Triple Net Lease (NNN) Investments (also called Mailbox Money)

Developing property includes a lot of risk, but high risk can generate high rewards. All development projects need upfront funding for due diligence costs, land acquisition, and construction. So, securing funds through partnerships or bank loans is a must. Establishing these financing relationship early on is key.

As noted above, commercial property development can yield high returns. A single development project can net six-figure profits—and often seven figure profits. The disadvantage is a project can take from several months to a few years to complete.

Let's get started on how to develop a single tenant property. You need to control one of two things—the tenant, or the property. You need the following *key* consultants:

- ***Real Estate Attorney***—to review title, leases, contracts, partnership agreements, and other legal documents

- ***Civil Engineer***—analysis of the physical site conditions, feasibility studies, land, utilities, easements, access, parking ratios, setbacks, and to create site plans

- *Architect*—designs and draw plans

- *General Contractor*—provide construction costs and builds any construction items called for in the lease

- *Title Company*—review property information and title searches

- *Environmental Company*—soils, ground water contamination, asbestos, and lead paint testing

Getting Started as a Developer—A Checklist for Your First Investment Property

- ✓ Chose a specific market area, and visit with City Economic Department

- ✓ Identify land parcel or building to acquire

- ✓ Research who owns the land or building—research county tax appraisal district records

- ✓ Call and meet with property owner to ask if they will sell property

- ✓ Request survey of the property and any other reports

- ✓ Send Letter of Intent to make an offer

- ✓ If Seller accepts offer, send purchase agreement

- ✓ Seller signs contract and then buyer signs contract

- ✓ Email signed contract to title company

- ✓ Title company will request earnest money to be placed in escrow (negotiate only $5,000) paid within three days after commencement date

- ✓ Find a credit tenant and negotiate Letter of Intent (LOI) offer

- ✓ Negotiate lease and execute signed lease by landlord and tenant

- ✓ Close on property

- ✓ Tenant constructs building

- ✓ Landlord collects rent

- ✓ Landlord holds on to property or sells

A triple net (NNN) lease (a lease where tenant is responsible for paying property taxes, insurance, and maintenance) is the best type of lease to maximize your investment. Investors like to purchase NNN leases because they just have to buy the property and collect rent checks—thus, the term "mailbox money." With a high credit tenant, leases can range from ten to twenty years with ten percent rent increases every five years.

With triple net lease investments, the most important thing is the risk reflected in the company's credit rating. Those companies with a rating of BBB and higher on the Standard and Poor's scale are considered "investment grade." Examples of companies with such ratings include: McDonald's, Walgreens, CVS, Starbucks, Chase Bank, etc.

Typically, you can charge rent that is ten percent of the purchase price. For example, if the land costs are $600,000 you can charge the tenant $60,000 in annual rent. Due to McDonald's credit in today's market, NNN McDonald's leases are selling for four percent cap rates (Cap Rate= Annual Net Operating Income/Cost).

Net Operating Income: $60,000
Estimated Value = $60,000 / 0.4% = $1,500,000

$1,500,000
$ 720,000 (minus cost for land, soft and hard costs)
$ 780,000 Profit

There is a lot more detail to developing property, but this represents a high-level overview of the process. My first development project was a five acre property in Tyler, Texas. There were two property owners with whom to negotiate. After more than one year working with them, they both decided to sell. Working with Sellers comes down to trust. This Seller had several other offers prior to the one my partners and I made, but he didn't trust any of the other buyers. This is where being upfront and honest pays off. We were working with one national tenant who had wanted a location at this site for years. My patience paid off! You have to have a lot of patience to develop property. We were able to do a build-a-suit for Walgreens, a ground lease with Chase Bank, and a ground lease with McDonald's on the property—a trifecta development project! It was a lot of hard work, road trips, negotiations, delays, but it was worth it. I still drive by the project today and know the old, 1950s motel is gone and new development has cleaned up the area and the local residents have a new place to shop, bank, and eat.

Commercial real estate is an exciting and always changing business. It is a tough and a very competitive industry. I am always surprised that it is dominated by men—and they don't even like to shop!

By the way, I never did become a famous actress, but in 1991, I did move to Los Angeles, CA. where I attended an acting school. I was on several TV shows and movies as an "extra," but never made it as an actress. I worked on a few TV shows as an assistant casting director, including "Melrose Place," "A League of Their Own" (yes, Penny Marshall is a hoot), and the George Forman Show. During my time in Los Angeles I was able to meet some famous people, including Barbara Streisand, Michael Jackson, Warren Beatty, Sean Penn, and Tom Hanks. I had a blast pursuing my dreams, and so will you! *Never, never, never, give up!*

About Pamela J. Goodwin

Pamela J. Goodwin is the founder of Dallas, TX based, Goodwin Commercial, where she specializes in developing retail and restaurant pad sites. Her experience spans more than two decades in project management, leasing, property development, due diligence, entitlement, and tenant representation. She's worked for several large shopping center developers including, The Hahn Co., Macerich, and General Growth Properties, and on the tenant-side with Brinker International, where she developed over fifty pad sites for free-standing Chili's and On the Border Restaurants.

Pamela's been featured in *BizNow*, *Texas Real Estate Business*, *Shopping Center Business*, and the *Dallas Business Journal*. She's a member of ICSC and Deals in Heels, and a licensed Texas Real Estate Broker. She's a graduate of the University of Nebraska-Lincoln, and a big Cornhusker football fan! Pamela is the author of *One Cent Lemonade to Million Dollar Deals-25 Jobs & 25 Lessons I Wish I Learned Sooner!*

Email: Pam@GoodwinCommercial.com
Website: GoodwinCommercial.com
LinkedIn: LinkedIn.com/in/pamgoodwin
Facebook: Facebook.com/pamela.z.goodwin

Chapter 5

"*No*" is the Beginning of the Conversation Especially When You Are Talking to an Economic Developer
by Jessica L. Herrera

When you think of economic development, the first thing that comes to mind may be an economist or a real estate developer of some sort. Economic development has many characteristics, including salesperson, connector, broker, ombudsman, and advocate. All are equally important and vital to the process. But, in the end, economic development is about selling your community. That is why "*No*" is just the ice breaker. These attributes are crucial in both the economic development profession and commercial real estate sector. Economic developers might not be selling one specific site or shopping center, but are in the business of selling our community. I remember when I first started my career in economic development and a former colleague shared that it is very important to always remember that "*No*" is just the beginning of the conversation.

I did not fully understand what that meant until I started realizing that as we sell our community, we are going to come across the word "no" dozens of times. I'll never forget my first phone call with a retailer/real estate representative, highlighting our market and talking about why they needed to expand in our city. The first immediate response was "No, we're not interested at this time." However, I kept insisting via multiple phone calls, emails, mailings, and face-to-face visits at industry-related shows and conferences. Those five to ten minutes of visits at industry trade shows go a long a way—especially if you can get them to remember your name and or just call you by your city. For me, I am often asked, "El Paso...so what's going on and why do we need to be there?" Once you've reached that level of recognition and response from the representative, you know it's not a matter of if, but when.

Finally, after numerous calls, proactive data collection sent via email, visits at conferences, followed by those incredibly important site visits in our community paid off. Those tools helped lead to identifying multiple site locations. I can clearly remember walking into their establishment on opening day, seeing the number of people employed, the long line wrapped around their site, and the excitement and anticipation brewing to see this tenant open its doors in our community. "Largest opening in the history of the chain," was what I heard from their team within a few short days of opening. I thought to myself, "That's what we've been trying to tell you all along!"

It is in our best interest to keep pushing forward and maintaining that level of persistence and determination because in the end, it will pay off dividends. This can also be translated into personal and professional areas. Maintaining perseverance is crucial. As we push forward, we build and strengthen relationships along the way that ultimately result in achieving success in our respective communities. Relationships are at the very core of what we do every day through continued interaction with intergovernmental entities, economic development partners, the community, and the private sector. Taking the time to personally write a thank you note to the individual(s) or organization(s) you come across every day goes a long way. Nowadays, we are so connected to our mobile devices, iPads, text messages, and emails that we hardly take the time to pick up the phone and have a conversation with someone and or meet them for a cup of coffee. Building and fostering those relationships is vital to the success of any project or initiative. Interestingly, usually most deals get done out of the office—and that is where these relationships are built and strengthened. I learned that in both economic development or in commercial real estate if you're not on the ground, at the site and understanding the area, then you cannot be successful.

These two industries are interconnected and you always have to be on the clock, working late hours, weekends, traveling, courting clients, hosting dinners, cocktail receptions, presenting at community events, etc. knowing that you never know who you will meet and can turn into a potential deal, prospect, and or simply connect with. Finding a balance between your career, your family, and friends and simply having some down time for yourself is always important to keep in mind. It's easier said than done, especially when you have a passion for what you do and it becomes a part of who you are every day, and no matter where you're at you will see things and places through a different lens. I find myself driving past a shopping center and taking a look at the tenant mix, looking at the neighborhood nearby, getting a sense for what type of employers are there, etc. Women for the most part are multi-taskers and can usually figure out a way to deal with multiple projects, different attitudes and personalities, and still figure out a way to get it done. From my perspective, it's important to transcend that passion and ability to all areas of your life.

A good meal brings people together. As a "foodie" myself, I learned connecting with people outside of the office. Additionally, going to meet contacts at their favorite restaurant or coffee shop or even place of business goes a long way. The experience we build with our prospects and clients should be one that leaves a lasting impression. I sometimes find myself on the golf course, at a basketball game, an art exhibit, a chamber of commerce reception or a 7:00 a.m. breakfast meeting with a community organization—all because relationships are crucial and they are not going to happen overnight. I call it "social engineering"—really understanding that success is contingent on your relationships with others. If a connection can be made—and the crucial follow-up is executed—success can be achieved.

Facilitating and guiding the real estate and development community through the regulatory process is also crucial. In economic development, you are both the advocate and the broker between these entities. It is important to develop a relationship with the commercial real estate community and understand their needs, challenges, and hurdles to getting a deal done. However, it is also important to understand how to navigate the regulatory environment and familiarize yourself with those individuals who will help you help your client(s). Time is money...and having a sense of urgency is critical to the success of any project. Constant communication and coordination with all stakeholders involved or affected will help to drive the project forward. It is usually easier said than done, but once you establish those relationships and identify what works best with each stakeholder, then you're able to clearly communicate any specific challenges or needs you have moving forward.

I had a grocery retailer contact me as they were working on store expansions and were having challenges with the city development office and some utilities. The real estate representative made it very clear that store opening was projected within two weeks and final permits and inspections (including utilities) needed to be set before operations could begin. Our conversation entailed everything from street bore, to fire suppression systems, to phone lines. Although I was not the expert on any of these areas, I made sure she knew I would navigate that process and assured her the opening date would take place as scheduled. As I hung up the phone, I realized the challenge of dealing with numerous entities, but knew it was not impossible. I immediately contacted the city department and began to identify where the issues were and how we were going to resolve them. I was sitting at a conference while this was happening and had no contact information for one of the utilities. I remember sitting across from a gentleman who looked over and said he overheard my conversation. He had a contact for the utility who is "the doer" (as he called him) and would help with anything.

Talk about being at the right place at the right time. After contacting the people to get things moving and inspections done, I realized I had a list of "doers." I knew that contact list would be my gold mine. After many phone conversations and email, we finally got the grocer to open as scheduled. It is very gratifying to see all the behind-the-scenes chaos behind me and realize the real estate representative knew she could count on me. Most importantly, she had confidence I could navigate that process and avoid taking her focus from other issues. As a result, this not only helped build the relationship, but also shed some light on how to resolve these issues, processes and/or areas internally to become more efficient and business friendly.

I've been fortunate to work with great people throughout my career. I remember one of my mentors would always tell me, *"Insert yourself and know that a person who never made a mistake also never tried anything new."* As a young professional woman, it is intimidating and an exciting time to be working in an industry filled with knowledgeable and experienced colleagues in economic development and real estate. However, I knew it was important to know I had to learn to speak up and be part of projects and initiatives that would expose me to the industry. This allows me to grow and forces me to get out of my comfort zone. One of my first board meetings was very intimidating as I had to present a project I was leading. The room was filled with predominantly C-Level male executives and I remember my palms were sweating. I was terrified to make a mistake. Then I realized I was trying something new and was passionate about it and had immersed myself in it. The worst thing that could happen was not knowing the answer to a question. At the end of the meeting, I looked around the room and realized that these people experienced the same thing at one point in their careers. I was fortunate to have the opportunity to work with them, as well as learn from them and begin to build a lasting relationship.

In life one needs to be bold and courageous to achieve success. There will be many times when you'll have to face a daunting task or take a risk and not know what the results will be. These moments in your life should be seen as an opportunity to put your best foot forward and really immerse yourself in the decision or task at hand with an understanding that although it may seem challenging it can also be very rewarding in the end. There have been two times in my life where I have accepted a job opportunity away from my hometown and in areas where I had neither close family nor friends. I remember thinking to myself if the decision was a good one, what sacrifices I would have to make by being away from my family etc. and in both instances these two experiences have been positively life changing. When you move forward on a decision or challenging project, there will always be unknowns and mistakes will be made along the way, but what's really important is how you get to know yourself better and understand where there may be room for improvement, what your strong suits are, and where your interests or passions lie. Building that intuitiveness for yourself is critical for both your personal and professional development. It's incredible how life takes you on a journey to places you've never imagined and the people you meet along the way become lifelong friends, colleagues, and mentors. "Attitude," as someone said to me, "determines altitude" and that always resonated with me everywhere I went as I knew that it's all about striving for a positive, collaborative, and determined way of thinking and doing, coupled with treating others with the respect and courtesy you would like to be treated. Collaboration is crucial in any industry, not only in economic development and commercial real estate, as it will build the foundation for any successful endeavor or project. As you're fostering and strengthening these relationships, building a strong support network of close personal and or professional friends or colleagues helps provide you with continuous encouragement, advice, and guidance that are instrumental to your life. You have to inspect what you expect. Live your life with faith. Don't doom it with a life dominated by doubt. Remember "No" indeed is the beginning of the conversation that through perseverance, dedication, and hard work will lead to a "let's visit" followed by "we're opening our doors on this date" which leads to a successful deal all done in heels!"

About Jessica L. Herrera

Jessica L. Herrera has more than eight years of economic development experience at the state, city, and international levels including expertise on business retention and expansion efforts, small business development, retail recruitment strategies, and successful marketing and communication initiatives. As Redevelopment Manager for the City of El Paso, Texas Economic Development Department, she works to build and strengthen public-private partnerships to rebuild key assets of the city that support mixed-use project development, historic preservation, and downtown redevelopment.

LinkedIn: LinkedIn.com/pub/jessica-herrera/45/aa4/39a

Chapter 6

Diary of a Dirt Sniffer
by Donna Johnson

How could I have known when I walked through the doors of Alan I. Jones Companies in 1972 that I had found my lifetime work and career? I had landed a position as the Administrative Assistant to the President and Chairman of the Board of the company, Jerry D. Fults and Alan I. Jones, respectively. Those of you who have been in the real estate business for a long while will recognize at least one of those names. Jerry Fults remained quite successful in commercial real estate until he passed away a few years ago. Alan Jones had been brought up in the real estate world by a gentleman named Henry S. Miller, Sr., and although I wasn't too real estate savvy, even *I knew* who Henry S. Miller, Sr. was. Alan had been one of Mr. Miller's top producers and Mr. Miller not only taught Alan a great deal about real estate, but Alan also learned from his example how to build a team of the best people possible, and how to earn their loyalty. Unfortunately, Alan Jones passed away long enough ago that his name may not be familiar to many of you, but he was well-respected and admired by his employees (and even his competitors).

I had no idea at the time that many of the "young pups" who worked for Alan would go on to become icons in the commercial real estate world. Another example of "greatness" that roamed our halls was our in-house counsel, Paul Pulliam. Several years later, Paul went on to form Safeco Land Title Company, and then on to run Republic Title Company for many more years until his retirement just a few years ago. I was surrounded by a group of people with dynamic personalities who loved working in real estate and I was right in the middle of it all. I was fortunate enough to witness "negotiating" at its finest. Alan and Jerry mentored hundreds of men and women throughout their careers and made a positive impact on the lives of many, including one Administrative Assistant . . . *me*! It was obvious and it could not be denied: I was hooked on the world of real estate!

Alan I. Jones Companies was a commercial real estate development company, but was also heavily involved in something called "land syndication." Our salesmen cold called on all the doctors, lawyers, and Indian chiefs they could find to give them the great opportunity to invest in joint ventures...somewhat speculative opportunities, in many cases. Eventually, the Securities and Exchange Commission decided that this kind of speculative activity was not necessarily beneficial to many of those investors, especially those who were less sophisticated, and the business of land syndication/joint venture, as we knew it, came to an end. We also developed several office buildings along with various other development projects. One project, in particular, was very exciting. Alan had managed to negotiate the purchase of the only lakefront property that was zoned for condominiums at a beautiful lake in Austin you may have heard of . . . Lake Travis! Again, I was able to witness his exceptional negotiating methods and I was in awe! We built a spectacular condominium development, The Bluffs at Lakeway, and I was fortunate enough to spend many weekends there watching our ace salesmen sell these gorgeous condominiums. They were selling like hotcakes and then something called a recession (my first to experience) came along. Overnight, it seemed, our bluffs were just that . . . a "bluff." Sadly, like many other companies, Alan I. Jones

Companies did not survive the recession; however, even in that time of uncertainty, I witnessed something that has stayed with me throughout my career. Although we were done—bankrupt—and about to close our doors, every person who worked for Alan I. Jones Companies showed up for work all or part of every day (with no promise of pay) for the two to three weeks it took to turn out the lights and lock our doors. I learned how important it is to develop loyalty, and I learned a little about how to develop loyalty in others, and to appreciate that loyalty. After that four-year experience, I was "hooked," but I was a divorced mom and we were still in a recession. As I started the search for a new "career," I was a little skeptical and leery of getting back in the same game. I felt I needed something a little safer than the adrenaline-pumping world of commercial real estate. Fortunately, having worked quite a bit with Paul (Pulliam), our in-house counsel at Alan I. Jones Companies, I had also developed a strong interest (and a fair amount of knowledge) in real estate law. So when an opportunity presented itself at a prominent Dallas law firm that specialized in real estate law, I took my real estate "expertise" and transformed myself into a legal secretary specializing, of course, in real estate! This was safe but also allowed me to continue working in the field I loved so much. It was now 1976 and a second professional mentor—Sam Glast—entered my life. Sam was one of *the best* real estate lawyers in Dallas and, although he has since retired, the firm that still bears his name (Glast, Phillips & Murray, P.C.) remains one of the best law firms around. The firm represented some very prestigious real estate developers, including several who were international, and I had the perfect opportunity to see some of the most amazing negotiating skills you could ever imagine, sometimes all the way to the closing table! This was an incredible experience . . . something safe *and* exciting. I continued my education at SMU and became a bona fide Real Estate Paralegal, and I was enjoying my new career immensely. One of our firm's clients was an exciting young company, an "upscale" fast food company called Grandy's Restaurants. It was now 1984. One day, Sam called me into his office and said he thought I had worked for him long enough! Obviously, I was puzzled by that statement and was certainly thinking the worst! You have to understand...Sam and I share the same birthday (we're both Sagittarians) and we are both left-handed, so we were a lot alike and his kind of humor seldom surprised me, yet this time it did. I was still a divorced mom and, needless to say, the thought of looking for another job at this juncture did not appeal to me. Fortunately, I was soon able to take a sigh of relief, as Sam explained to me that Grandy's was looking for someone to join their company to do "site selection and acquisitions" and they had approached Sam to let him know they were interested in *me*! It was a tough decision to make but, with a slight push out the door from Sam, I moved on...alas, a dirt sniffer was about to be born! Sam and I have remained close friends all these years; however, when one of his lawyers is counsel for the other side on a deal I'm negotiating and I mention that *"Sam taught me everything I know about negotiating,"* I do sometimes find his or her reaction quite humorous!

Without a doubt, I was a little apprehensive about the new job ahead of me; however, mentor number three stepped in and saved the day. Millard Wright, one of the kindest and smartest people with whom I have had the pleasure of working, welcomed me to his team and taught me everything I could ever hope to know about how to select the best locations for Grandy's. Equally important, Millard taught me the value of "win-win" negotiating. That lesson serves me well to this day, as I truly believe when the parties walk away with the sense that the negotiations have been fair to all, you are much more likely to get the first phone call for the next site you might want. To this day, I remember two other important things that Millard taught me: one, *"I'm not in the real estate business— I'm in the restaurant (or retail or bank) business."* That is to say, you do not just select and acquire the "real estate," you stay involved and engaged, seeing the job all the way through, until that real estate becomes the best restaurant or retail or bank location it can be," and two, *"When you make a u-turn, put the rock in your other pocket!"* Now, that one takes a little explaining, doesn't it? You have to understand, I was eventually good enough at reading a map (we actually used paper ones "back then!") that you could have dropped me in the desert with one and I could have found my way—in the dark—to anywhere in the continental United States, *but* initially I had some "directional" issues when I was writing things on the map (yes, we actually did that "back then," as well!). Millard's hint was for me to visualize that when I was driving and made a u-turn and began to write things on the map I "put the rock in my other pocket." The scary thing is, it worked. I will not ever admit it, but there might have been a time or two when I actually had a rock in my pocket! I also learned how to calculate percentage rent (with both a natural and artificial breakpoint!), to put dots on maps, draw site sketches, grid markets, do traffic counts, create site plans, run proformas and IRRs, and how to "win-win" negotiate with all types of people...those who were fairly unsophisticated in real estate matters, like the "mom and pop" who owned a nice corner property, and those who were some of the most sophisticated developers around at the time. Most importantly, I learned to treat people fairly, to keep your word, and to respect the relationships you form.

I have never looked back, but each time I have looked forward to a new opportunity, I have remembered the many important things I learned from these three mentors. I have now enjoyed the site selection/acquisitions "gig" for over thirty years. I have survived a couple more recessions and have been fortunate enough to do the job I love for some really good companies (Grandy's twice, Payless ShoeSource, Jack in the Box, Wachovia/Wells Fargo, and currently Capital One). Each position with each company has been rewarding in many ways and challenging in other ways. One of the greatest rewards is the fact that I've been able to forge professional relationships with some of the best people on the planet (I really believe that). Many of those relationships have withstood the test of time, and I have carried them with me from company to company. As a bonus, I am lucky enough to still call many of those men and women friends.

One challenge, of course, is negotiating the most favorable positions possible for your company on critical issues (having co-tenancy and exclusive protections, and NOT having covenants to open and continuous operation clauses!). I am often asked how I am able to negotiate some of the favorable positions that I do on these and other important issues in ground (or inline) leases. I can only say that I believe this is where the fairness = relationship = partnership = better understanding of each party's needs is very valuable. For example, listening and understanding a landlord's need for a tenant's commitment but being able to hold firm on not having a covenant to open by way of an agreement to commence (or even complete) construction with a deadline to do so (and a recapture right for landlord) is often an acceptable position for a landlord. When a landlord has a "policy" of giving no co-tenancy or exclusive protection, continuing the discussions with various fallback positions that result in *some* level of protection almost always works...maybe the protection has time or other limitations, but being able to get some protection is better than getting none at all. I try never to use the term "deal killer." I may infer it, but I always indicate that word is *not* in my vocabulary and I don't want to add it! Then I get back in there with a good fallback position and hope I don't have to use that "new word!" Of course, you always have to promise the landlord/developer that you'll *never* divulge that they made an exception and gave you what you needed on those various provisions . . . you know, it *might* just ruin their reputation for being "difficult," right?

The bottom line is you can still be firm, but you can also be nice. People generally like to work and "do deals" with people they like. I have heard that more than once from a developer or landlord. If they like you and know they'll be treated fairly, why wouldn't they rather call you first than call someone who they don't like as much? A deal is a deal, but working through it with someone you like dealing with *can and does make a difference*! I recently received the "first call" on three highly coveted corner locations in the Dallas market as opportunities for Capital One. Forging these relationships year after year, each party treating the other fairly through "win-win" negotiations, and carrying those relationships with you throughout your career...I believe that truly is the winning edge.

The other great reward and exciting thing I think we see now in commercial real estate is that more and more women are being recognized for their talents in this business and they are prospering accordingly. Obviously, when I began this journey in the early seventies, this was a totally male-dominated profession. At Alan I. Jones—where it all began for me—there was *one* female salesperson! But I remember her name to this day—Jo Wilson—not only because she was a female in that male-dominated profession, but because she eventually became *the number one salesperson* at Alan I. Jones Companies.

While I am no match for any of the three mentors who made such an impact on my life, I have tried to pass my experiences (both good and bad) and my "wisdom" and insight on to others along the way, all in the hope that they can enjoy their life in the real estate world as much as I enjoy mine. I still have a lot to learn but, hopefully, there's still a lot of time for me to learn it! Who knows, if I'm lucky, maybe I'll still be in the site selection business in the hereafter, hopefully sniffing some Heavenly dirt for some terrific restaurant or retailer or bank!

On a personal note, my first mentor, Alan I. Jones, was undoubtedly one of the most special people I have ever known. I was going through a rough time—my (first!) divorce—at the time I went to work for him. I was a divorced mom and uncertain of what my future held, but I was determined to provide the best life possible for my daughter and me. Alan went the extra mile to give me a boost in that direction. He co-signed for my first car (a 1970 Dodge Dart, Demon in baby blue), and on more than one occasion he gave me an advance on my salary so that I could buy diapers and baby food. He also allowed me to bring my daughter, Shelly, to the office on Saturdays so I could work (and get paid for!) overtime but still have her with me. Most especially, Alan taught me that persistence and perseverance, above all else, get you where you want to be.

Alan had four framed pieces of motivational artwork on his wall for all the years I knew him. Alan's wife, Marty Jones, and I continued our friendship long after Alan's death. Several years after he passed away, Marty sent all four framed pieces to me . . . and I have them in my office today. I would like to share them with you:

"Many people can be responsible for your success, but only you are responsible for your failure." -Unknown

"Life is short, fragile, and does not wait for anyone. There will never be a more perfect time than now to pursue your dreams and goals." -Unknown

"Patience, persistence, and perseverance make an unbeatable combination for success." -Napoleon Hill

"When you want to succeed as badly as you want to breathe, then you will be successful." -Eric Thomas

About Donna Johnson

Donna Johnson is a lifetime resident of Dallas, Texas. She grew up in Oak Cliff, where she still lives with her husband, Joe Warner, who is also a Dallas and Oak Cliff native. Donna graduated from Sunset High School and SMU. Her daughter and two grandchildren live close-by and are the loves of her life.

Donna and Joe are heavily involved in dog rescue/fostering/adoption/education/spay-neuter activities, and she has also been permitted for over twenty years by the State of Texas as a Wildlife Rehabilitator, nursing injured and orphaned wildlife back to health for release back into the wild.

Other community activities include being a Big Sis with Big Brothers, Big Sisters, as well as a member of the Board of Directors for the Dance Council of North Texas and the Sunset High School Alumni Association. Donna was nominated as a Woman of Inspiration in Dallas/Ft. Worth in 2008 by Bea's Kids in recognition of her community involvement. Bea's Kids is an outstanding charitable organization founded in Dallas by Bea Salazar in 1990, with the mission to provide educational and personal development programs to children from low-income families to encourage them to stay in school, and thus break the cycle of poverty.

Donna has over thirty years in commercial real estate site selection, negotiation, acquisition, development, property management, and the disposition of properties/assets (for five major companies).

LinkedIn: LinkedIn.com/pub/donna-johnson/39/825/343

Chapter 7

The Sky is the Limit
by Gwen MacKenzie

Shopping center real estate brokerage is a field with enormous possibilities for women. It allows you to control your destiny, select your clients, choose your co-workers, set your own schedule (to accommodate carpools and kids' soccer matches), and earn an unlimited income—what you are worth (the same as men) with no glass ceiling.

I am in the shopping center development and brokerage industry, and every time I drive by a shopping center there is a potential for me to do business with the owners of that property. While I don't spend my working hours "shopping"— as some of my friends suspect—I do use everyday errands like buying groceries or dropping off dry cleaning as an opportunity to gather "intel" that I can use in business and in developing relationships with investors, including those right in my neighborhood.

Retail or shopping center real estate brokerage (i.e. leasing shop space to retailers, representing tenants looking for shop space or handling the sales/acquisition of shopping center investments) is typically a one-hundred percent commission career. Historically, women have not been comfortable in a commission-only environment—a dynamic that has worked against them and often kept them from one of the top areas for women to make significant income and have great autonomy in their life. But history is changing, and more and more women are refining and applying key abilities and skill sets that allow them to enter and excel in the shopping center real estate industry. I touch on some of these skills below.

Sales/Business Development

You cannot manage, sell, or lease a shopping center until you persuade a client to let you handle their investment asset.

Financial Acumen

Virtually all properties are owned as investments, and investors expect a return that meets or exceeds the industry average. An understanding of accounting practices, financial statements, and property valuation is crucial for advancing in this field.

Aesthetic Sense

The creation of a shopping center is about invoking a sense of place. Shopping centers are successful when their developers create an environment where people want to visit and shop—a combination of architecture, landscaping, ambiance, accessibility, signage and, most important, a mix of retailers who will attract the highest amount of shoppers and generate the highest percentage of sales for their particular neighborhood.

Construction/Property Management

Shopping centers are bricks and mortar. You have to build them and manage them. So an understanding of construction and maintenance is crucial, no matter what discipline of retail commercial real estate you elect to pursue.

Building a Career

My ascension in the retail real estate industry was not a straight journey from point A to point B, but rather a series of ventures—some by strategy, some by good fortune, but all based on my own sweat equity and willingness to master every aspect of this profession.

Property Management

I was working as an administrative assistant for the President of a development company, and quickly came to the attention of the Property Manager by frequently making queries about aspects of her job. When this individual left for an opportunity elsewhere, she recommended I take over her position—a role that oversees rent collection, prepares financial statements, maintains operations of the shopping center, and enforces lease provisions. During my tenure as a Property Manager, I interacted with leasing agents who showed space to prospective tenants and negotiated the terms for their lease in the center. I also volunteered to handle renewal negotiations for our existing tenants and, after becoming comfortable with that responsibility, I transitioned to the role of leasing agent full time.

Leasing Agent

As a leasing agent, I budgeted for planned leasing for my client's centers, including the cost to build-out space for retailers. I regularly canvassed the area, visiting stores and attempting to persuade the storeowners to relocate or open a second location in the shopping centers I leased. I called retailers I saw on TV commercials, in newspaper ads, or while visiting other areas. I showed space and negotiated lease terms. When the industry trade organization—International Council of Shopping Centers—launched a Certified Leasing Specialist (CLS) professional designation, I was in the first class to earn the certification. Eventually, I advanced to handling large regional malls and power centers for major institutional clients. I had strong relationships with major grocery companies who leased space, as well as the top retailers in the country.

Investment Brokerage

Investors of shopping centers generally buy and sell their investments within a ten-year period. While leasing centers, I was able to assist and participate in a number of these sales with the investment brokers who handled the transactions. I decided I would enjoy selling shopping centers, and I felt my background in property management, and as a leasing agent, provided me with a competitive advantage in identifying and selling the benefits of a particular shopping center to prospective investors. So I resigned from my great job leasing some of the top shopping centers in Southern California, and jumped into a new adventure.

After meeting with the nation's top national brokerage firms, I selected one and launched my new career. The first order of business was to identify a territory and profile every shopping center in that area. I took pictures of each center, and became familiar with the tenants, the construction, and the benefits and challenges of each property. Once I was familiar with each property, I had to research and locate their owners, and find their contact information so that I could connect with them.

After I identified and researched around four-hundred shopping centers, I spent my first year calling and meeting with their owners. My goal was to establish a relationship with them, provide them with my opinions on their centers, and make sure they knew I was interested in helping them when they decided to sell. Because of my previous experience, I had a head start over those who were transitioning from another field or just out of college. My experience in leasing gave me confidence to intelligently discuss the assets and how they would be perceived by retailers. I also knew the major players—developers, investors, and institutions—since I had been working in the industry, frequently attending events and networking. In order to increase my profile and bring attention to my new career path, I authored articles in industry publications, volunteered as a speaker, chaired panels, and was often interviewed as an expert in retail real estate.

During my second year as an investment broker, I earned a fairly sizeable listing, and fortunately, I was able to sell it rather quickly at a great price. Several other listings followed this success, and my satisfied clients gave me substantial repeat business. I never took the business for granted and tried to stay true to the activities that made me successful. I stayed on the phones, constantly calling everyone I knew, and I kept meeting with owners at their office, for lunch or coffee, or at industry events. I loved my "job"—primarily interacting with investment-minded sellers or buyers and discussing their shopping centers.

Institutional Acquisitions

In 2006, one of the nation's top Real Estate Investment Trusts (REITS), owner of a substantial portfolio of shopping centers and mixed-use projects on both coasts, hired me to handle their West Coast acquisition program. I was meeting with the same shopping center owners as before, only instead of trying to get the listing to sell their property, I was now attempting to persuade them to let me acquire the property. Since this was a publicly traded company, the financial analysis required to acquire shopping centers was rigorous, and the due diligence process demanded careful investigation of the title, construction, leases, and financial statements, as well as monitoring environmental issues. Further, I had to plan the asset strategy going forward, including redevelopment, construction upgrades, and adjustments to the tenant mix, or any other major changes.

Coach & Mentor

As President of Brokerage Services for a national shopping center developer, I led a team of twenty investment brokers, leasing agents, and tenant rep brokers leasing more than fifteen million square feet in twelve states. My focus switched from personal participation in transactions, to guiding, mentoring, training, and coaching the brokerage team so they could achieve their goals. In addition, I was charged with generating new business using my relationships and my experience implementing a sales strategy to reach clients who were a good fit for the company's capabilities. At this point in my career, ICSC awarded me the professional designation of Certified Retail Property Executive (CRX).

Business Owner

In 2014 I launched a commercial real estate development firm called Creative Structures & Spaces. Our company tag line is "Creating Bricks & Mortar for the Creative Set." The focus of the company is mixed-use development, redevelopment, adaptive reuse, urban environments, live/work lofts, lifestyle centers, and specialty retail. The buildings and spaces we conceive are designed to meet the needs of artistic and creative users including art galleries, home furnishings showrooms, cowork and creative offices, culinary concepts, architectural and interior design firms, media and tech companies, gourmet grocers, fashion boutiques, and performing arts venues. Creative Structures & Spaces combines my expertise in all disciplines of commercial real estate with my life-long passion for the arts community.

A Few Words Of Wisdom

- Never miss an opportunity to go someplace where you can meet new people. Whether it is an industry networking event, an economic forecast, a ball game, or a housewarming, always attend. I make it a point to meet three new people at every event, and for a major industry trade show gain at least twenty new contacts.

- Don't be afraid to say you don't know the answer. Even the most accomplished industry professionals cannot keep abreast of everything happening in the market. If you are asked a question and you don't know the answer, don't fake it. Simply state that you will research and obtain the information requested. Then get back to the client promptly with the answers to their queries.

- Help your colleagues when they are out of work. Commercial real estate is a cyclical business. During downturns, some aspects such as development may slow down, and people can be laid off. It is important to stay in touch with those looking for work. Take your colleague to lunch, make calls on their behalf, and arrange introductions. It is the right thing to do, and the job seeker will remember and appreciate your efforts.

- Be aware of what your competitors are doing, but don't let fear or intimidation keep you from pursuing your dreams. There is always room for a new talent or new vision in the commercial real estate industry. Clients choose their brokers and commercial real estate advisors as much on trust and personality as they do on capability and track record. When I was first in investment brokerage, I was able to win business competing against major established players from national firms. I attribute this to my careful homework and research, and enthusiastically presenting my strategy, backed up by facts. You can win business by being more attentive and more focused than your competitors, or sometimes just by having a better connection on a personal level.

- Get outside the office and drive your markets. You cannot successfully understand the shopping center business from behind your desk, staring at the computer, or even talking on the phone. You must see your centers to understand them, and see the competing centers in the immediate trade area to compare the attributes of each.

- Become an expert in a particular niche of the industry. For much of my career, I was known for expertise with neighborhood grocery-anchored shopping centers and nationally anchored power centers. I knew the financial strength of each retailer, their prototypes and their merchandise, store sales volumes, as well as the competitive advantages and disadvantages of each retailer in that sector.

- Treat everyone with respect and courtesy. Our industry is small and you will do business with the same people again and again, although they may be in a different position. Never badmouth your competitors. It reflects poorly on your judgment. Protect your reputation above all—it is irreplaceable.

- Focus on relationships, not on the deal. Deals can—and often do—fall through, but relationships can continue for your whole career and lead to many more deals down the line.

- A lot of important decisions are made in the industry as a result of presentations. So spend time on this critical aspect of winning or strengthening a client relationship.

A Bit More on Presentations

Presentations are needed for a multitude of reasons in this industry—to solicit business or listings, to support budget requests, or to propose new development or proposed redevelopments, to name a few. Always have a contingency plan for every presentation, and think it out before you need to. What if you are giving a presentation and the power goes out or your computer crashes? Bring some hard copies of your presentation just in case. What if one of your colleagues or teammates (the architect, the leasing broker) is unable to attend the presentation at the last minute or is caught in traffic? Identify in advance who knows the material and can fill in for their section. I also still believe in doing a dress rehearsal (probably a throw back from my days as a dancer) before an important meeting. Sometimes we all have to "wing it," but I believe in keeping those situations to a minimum.

After a presentation or important meeting, always circle back with team members and review what went right, what went wrong, and what needs to be improved. It is always amazing to me to hear the different perceptions that individual team members have after a meeting. And ask the clients who viewed your presentation to give you feedback and commentary (sometimes they will need to wait until the whole process is completed).

Gratitude to Those Who Came Before Me

The commercial real estate industry has provided me with incredible opportunities and a group of talented, energetic, enthusiastic colleagues and friends. I feel deeply privileged to have worked under some of the top players in the industry.

At Donahue Schriber, which was owned by industry icons Dan Donahue and Tom Schriber, I learned to form strong relationships with retailers, and I was often reminded that the landlords need the retailers, and the retailers need the landlords. Dan and Tom also taught me that it was okay to disagree with company leadership and still have a respectful dialogue about the positions of each party. Most important, Dan and Tom ran a company that was really fun. It was a joy to come to work each day.

Candace Rice, the Senior Vice President of Leasing at Donahue Schriber, was a well-known industry executive and one of the founding members of ICSC's Certified Leasing Specialist committee. An incredible proponent for the shopping center industry, she was a wonderful mentor. I can remember going to her many times when I was overwhelmed and she would say, "Don't worry. It will all get done. It always does." And she was right.

At Sperry Van Ness, I was able to interact directly with firm founders Rand Sperry and Mark Van Ness. Mark believed that you should start a commissioned investment brokerage career with one year's worth of savings. If you had less than one year, you risked not making it to the finish line. If you had more than one year's worth of savings, you might lack the drive to be successful in commissioned brokerage. Rand gave great advice on qualifying your clients to be sure they were serious and committed, before you devote precious time to assisting them. Rand and Mark were industry leaders in launching a firm that is based on full cooperation (sharing commissions) with all other brokers in the industry. This was proven to be beneficial to clients, providing a much higher level of activity and more aggressive pricing due to competition. Many firms followed this lead and I believe in their philosophy of cooperation today.

Finally, I am deeply grateful to have worked under Jeffrey Berkes, the President of the West Coast for REIT Federal Realty Investment Trust. From the intricacies of institutional financial underwriting, to how to write a proper letter (which I somehow must have missed in college), I use the lessons I learned from Jeff every day of my career. He warned me that my excessive use of exclamation points in correspondence affected my credibility (so I stopped using them right away!!!) Jeff also showed a deep commitment to helping colleagues in the industry, and always returned calls despite having a significant amount of responsibility for a prestigious publicly traded company.

Challenges for the Future

There is no question that the Internet and its shopping convenience has had an impact on the shopping center industry, and will continue to do so. The demise of the movie theater was predicted when at-home videos became available, yet patrons continue to flock to movies for the full experience. I think that the same is true for shopping centers. More than a shopping location, shopping centers have become a place where people gather, recharge, enjoy their surroundings, and spend quality time with their family. I know the shopping center industry will devote even more focus to defining and enhancing this experience—ensuring that the shopping center continues to hold a strong place in the heart of tomorrow's consumers.

About Gwen MacKenzie

Gwen MacKenzie, CRX, CLS, is a commercial real estate veteran with over twenty-five years of shopping center experience. She has closed over one billion dollars in transactions, and has expertise in acquisitions, investment sales, brokerage, leasing, asset management, development, redevelopment, construction management, and marketing of retail properties. Ms. MacKenzie was named to the Los Angeles Business Journal list of "Who's Who in Retail Real Estate Development." She graduated cum laude from Pepperdine University's George L. Graziadio School of Business & Management in Malibu, CA.

Website: ShopCenCRE.com
Website: CreativeStructuresCRE.com

I

Chapter 8

Be Present in All Things
by Jennifer K. Pierson

The theme of this section of the book is "be present in all things." It sounds like a lesson in psychology but it is not (or maybe it is). It is the only theme I know of that points to greatness in all things. It can be said and described in many different ways: when athletes are present in their sport they call it "being in the zone." Writers call it "a flash of brilliance," which is the opposite of writers block. Songs have expressed it with lyrics such as, "*Dance with the one that brought you*" (Shania Twain). We have all received the mass email with the quote, "*Today is a gift. That is why it is called the present.*" Others have said, "*Be true to who you are,*" or "*All we have is this moment.*" Maya Angelou wrote, "*Be present in all things and grateful in all things.*" Buddhists call this a state of "enlightenment." Across the globe and in every language exists this idea of being present.

However, being present seems to be the last thing we are aware of in our daily lives. Have you ever driven home from work or the grocery store and not remembered the drive? You were so deep in thought about the past or the future that you missed the entire drive.

As I type this now, in the back of my mind I am thinking, "*I wonder how many emails are piling up as I write this.*" "*I hope my kids eat a good lunch.*" "*How many calls do I need to make before I leave today?*" "*Is my team tracking comps correctly?*" "*That movie last night was really good.*" All of those thoughts are happening, and they are distracting me from writing this piece. And here is what it would look and feel like if I were really present: woman typing at desk, sensation of keys under fingers, thoughts about this piece flowing in my mind and my hands just type them. Chair is supporting me. Warm tea is next to me. I am perfectly content in this moment and so grateful. In this state of being present, all things are possible. My mind is centered. Creativity can reach new levels. I am calm. If this state can be achieved in all things, I am convinced we can achieve greatness beyond our wildest expectations.

Once I was running in a mini-triathlon and a man was coaching his wife while she was racing. She was racing for the prize money, I was just trying to finish. While we were running, the husband would say *"Stay calm," "Be calm," "Relax,"* which I found to be an odd coaching mantra because our bodies were in full motion and, in my case, stressed. How is she supposed to be calm while running up this dirt hill? And then I tried it . . . and I realized that he was exactly right. Once I calmed myself down (my mind and my body), I felt more efficient with the energy that I was using, and ultimately, I performed better. I believe this to be applicable to every single area of our lives.

Decide What You Want

Sit in a quiet place, clear your mind, try to stop all the thoughts going on in the background, and get in touch with your gut (for me, my "gut" is the real, authentic me). What is it you really want to do with your days? What will bring you joy? Do you love running numbers and would like the challenge of doing that every day? Are you great with people and would like to interact with lots of different people on a daily basis? Don't labor over it, just sit with it. Whatever you chose is the right choice. There are no mistakes.

Make a Plan

Planning is an important part of accountability and success. I find it impossible to have any direction in my life if I have not sat down and given myself space to explore where I want to go. A plan gives me action steps and allows me to be present in my daily life. A plan helps me to eliminate all the chatter in my mind and focus on the task at hand. I don't have to worry about the next five tasks because they are all laid out for me. I can dance with the one who brought me, and execute to the best of my ability on what I have planned to do for that moment.

In November of every year, I leave my office for a full day and head to the Four Seasons hotel. I let my team know I am going off the grid for the entire day. I don't answer any emails or phone calls. I sit at a beautiful table with a plug close by, and I get to work. I start with a blank piece of paper and brainstorm on the things I want to accomplish in the following year. I then take those thoughts and weave them into goals. These are usually goals for me as a team leader, goals for my personal revenue, goals for my team revenue, goals for systems on our team, goals for client events, etc. Then, I outline specific and measurable action steps that I believe it will take for me to reach those goals. I am an investment sales broker and I sell shopping centers. My business plan is like a map. It takes me on a journey through the upcoming year. If I want to sell twenty shopping centers in a year, I break down every step in the process. If I want to secure one listing per week, how many calls do I need to make? My map looks something like this:

- I want to sell twenty properties.

- What is my close ratio (how many listings do I need to sell twenty properties in a year)? My close ratio is very high because I have been selling shopping centers for a long time, but delays happen. People decide not to sell, transactions get pushed into the following year, etc. Therefore, I estimate I need thirty listings in order to sell twenty in a calendar year.

- To secure thirty listings in a year, I need to secure 2.5 listings per month.

- How many calls do I need to make in a month to secure 2.5 listings? I estimate, and I secure a listing from one out of every twenty calls. My formula is:

2.5 desired listings x 20 calls = 50 calls per month

That is an average of 2.5 calls per day (taking out the weekends).

For someone new in our business—let's say a rookie named Lucy—here is what the numbers will look like:

- Goal: Lucy wants to sell seven properties in a year. This will take twelve to twenty-four months of ramp up time, depending on Lucy's charisma and the state of the market.

- Close ratio: 3 to 1; meaning Lucy will sell one of every three properties she takes to market. In order to sell seven properties in a year, Lucy will need to list twenty-one.

- To secure twenty-one listings in a year, Lucy will need to list 1.75 properties per month.

- Lucy estimates she secures one listing out of every fifty calls he makes. With the goal of 1.75 listings per month, Lucy will need to make 87.5 calls per month. That is approximately 4.4 calls per day. However, Lucy does not want to wait twelve to twenty months to secure twenty-one listings so she is making around fifty calls per week, which equals ten per day.

Now back to our original theme of being present in all things. When you are making these calls, be present with each one. The goal is not to make one while thinking about the forty-nine others you need to make; the goal is to be present and connected with each call. Really hear what the other person on the line is saying. Listen to what they need. Connect with them. The way to make a lot of money (if that is your goal), is to help other people make a lot of money. Additionally, we all want to do business with people we trust. I personally trust people I connect with. So, "*dance with the one that brought you*" and when you are on a call, be on that call. Don't be looking at your computer; don't be thinking about other things you need to be doing. If you do those things, you might as well hang up the phone, because it is a waste of time. Quiet your mind of distracting thoughts, and be there.

In addition to cold calling goals, I have many other professional and personal goals: client events; building our database; canvassing comps; roadshow visits; eating well; being a good mom; exercising; spending time with my husband; staying grateful; investing; managing expenses; etc. On my November-day at the Four Seasons, I spend time on each of these subjects. Each subject gets a blank piece of paper, and from there, my goals almost write themselves. The goal must be specific, and I must be able to measure it. It also must be realistic and achievable within a certain timeframe. For instance, *"Make more calls"* does not work for me. Instead, I would use: *"Starting on January 1, 2014, call five people a day, every weekday, for two months. My targets are those who own retail shopping centers, starting in the city of Grapevine, and moving out to Southlake, when necessary."*

In order to realize these goals, I put them on an excel spreadsheet and I look at them every day. The first tab on my to-do spreadsheet is called "Today." I have a section for each weekday, and under each weekday, slots starting at 7:00 a.m. in fifteen-minute increments. I have a task in each time slot. Below is an example of a typical day:

Monday	
7:00 a.m.	tea and read goals
7:15 a.m.	tea and read goals
7:30 a.m.	tea and read goals
7:45 a.m.	check hard copy comps—put in spreadsheet
8:00 a.m.	call Joe on Main Street deal
8:15 a.m.	return calls
8:30 a.m.	return calls
8:45 a.m.	return calls
9:00 a.m.	return calls
9:15 a.m.	work on ICSC meetings
9:30 a.m.	work on ICSC meetings
9:45 a.m.	review signed OM's on Plaza Creek
10:00 a.m.	review signed OM's on Plaza Creek
10:15 a.m.	review signed OM's on Plaza Creek
10:30 a.m.	team meeting
10:45 a.m.	team meeting
11:00 a.m.	team meeting

11:15 a.m.	team meeting
11:30 a.m.	call owners around Richards Plaza
11:45 a.m.	call owners around Richards Plaza
12:00 noon	call owners around Richards Plaza
12:15 p.m.	eat at desk- clear out emails
12:30 p.m.	eat at desk- clear out emails
12:45 p.m.	eat at desk- clear out emails
1:00 p.m.	eat at desk- clear out emails
1:15 p.m.	give team instruction on dashboard to-dos
1:30 p.m.	give team instruction on dashboard to-dos
1:45 p.m.	give team instruction on dashboard to-dos
2:00 p.m.	send thank you notes to TBS people
2:15 p.m.	send thank you notes to TBS people
2:30 p.m.	send thank you notes to TBS people
2:45 p.m.	download audible book for car
3:00 p.m.	work on book writing
3:15 p.m.	work on book writing
3:30 p.m.	work on book writing
3:45 p.m.	work on book writing
4:00 p.m.	work on comps
4:15 p.m.	work on comps
4:30 p.m.	work on comps
4:45 p.m.	work on comps
5:00 p.m.	run numbers on North Plaza
5:15 p.m.	run numbers on North Plaza
5:30 p.m.	get listing signed on Heavens Square
5:45 p.m.	have Sarah book reservations for Sat. night
6:00 p.m.	clear out emails
6:15 p.m.	clear out emails
6:30 p.m.	clear out emails
6:45 p.m.	get ready for tomorrow

The second tab is called "Personal." If I think of anything during the day that I need to do on a personal front, it goes in that tab. If a personal thought is distracting me from my current task, I write it here and bring my attention back to the present. The third tab is called "Brokerage." If I think of someone I need to call or something I need to do for work, I put it on that tab. Again, once I write it down, I don't have to think about it and I can focus on my present task. The next tab is called "Team Meeting." The next three tabs are goals. They are 2014 Goals (or current year), Five-Year Goals, and Life Goals. I read all seven tabs every morning.

Because the document is in Excel, it is very easy for me to move things around and prioritize. And, because each of my daily tasks is time sensitive (they have a designated time slot), I execute each one with energy and purpose. Excel also has a "strike through" button, and it feels great to cross something off. Because of this system, it is very rare that I get to the end of a day that I feel like I haven't accomplished anything.

Execute

I used to think success could only come from stress and fear. I no longer believe this is true. I think people can be successful using fear and stress as a motivator, but I think we can be much, much more successful when we are calm, centered, and focused. I love how I feel when I am in a zone, achieving a goal with a calm sense of focus. I really dislike how I feel in a state of stress and anxiety, when I am just pushing through something to get it over with. And, I am certain that my results are better in the zone than in the state of anxiety. I also find I can get in a zone with virtually everything I do if I allow myself to be present in the moment.

Now here's the thing, all this "stay focused" and "be in the moment" discussion does not mean that being successful is without hard work. The trick is to enjoy the hard work. I find the only way to enjoy the hard work is to be present for it. Nevertheless, let's talk about the framework for hard work.

I find there is an exact correlation between working many hours, and success in commercial real estate. I have never seen a consistently successful broker who does not work long hours on a regular basis. In our office, we highlight the top twenty brokers (out of about 160) every year. On this elite list, we see the same people year after year. These professionals, without exception, put in long hours on the job. That is just the way it works.

A Few Tips for Executing

1. Every decision you make matters. When you have the choice of doing something now or later, get in the habit of doing it now. Something else will always come up later to get in the way of doing it then. I am not saying to do one more thing that makes you late for a client meeting. Be smart about it. When you have the choice without damaging consequences, do it.

2. Your time is all you have. If you choose to have a personal conversation at work, then be mindful of that choice. Be aware of socially talking with someone who is on a different time schedule than you. If the conversation is going long and you want to get back to work, excuse yourself. It is such an easy thing to do, but too many of us allow ourselves to be held hostage and resent it later. It is actually kinder to be honest and let the other person know that you need to get back to work.

3. Be a sponge without an ego. When you are young and think you should know more, don't let that thought get the best of you. You are young; this is the exact right time to ask a lot of questions and soak up all the information you possibly can. When you are more experienced on the job, it is still the exact right time to ask lots of questions and soak up all the information you possible can; and when you are the boss, it is still the exact right time to ask lots of questions and soak up all you can. The love of learning is a gift, and it will serve you well in everything you do. This mindset keeps you humble, and this is a great thing as well.

4. Steer clear of being entitled. This one can sneak up on us with thoughts like, *"I have been here for ten years; I deserve that referral."* For new people in the business it can be especially tricky. Look at it this way: every day, every moment you get to spend at your office is a gift. If there are people around you with more experience, watch them and learn from them. We are so lucky that others have gone before us and can teach us. If I am at my office until 8:00 p.m., how lucky I am to get to be in that environment. I see younger people getting into trouble with an attitude of *"I worked twelve hours today and didn't get any overtime."* If you are on a path to be a broker, there is no overtime. And every moment you get to be at your office to learn is a gift and a step towards your success; be grateful for it.

5. Make the calls. The difference between successful brokers and unsuccessful brokers is this: the first pick up the phone often and the second do not. I know of a broker in California who was wildly successful—let's

call her Beth. Beth was speaking to twenty-five or so brokers in her firm about her success. Most the brokers in the audience had at some point felt, or even said, "*If I had Beth's database, I could be that successful, too.*" So, Beth gave them all a copy, and in doing so she said, "*It does not worry me a bit that each of you has a copy of my database, because you won't use it . . . you won't pick up the phone and call.*"

6. Finally, enjoy yourself. If I could give one piece of advice to my younger self it would be to slow down, look around, and enjoy myself. I would say to my younger self, be grateful for what you have, because it is a lot. Work hard and enjoy it. Be honest about who you are and what you feel. I think Maya Angelou said it best: "*Be present in all things and grateful in all things.*"

About Jennifer Pierson

Jennifer Pierson is a retail investment specialist with CBRE, serving retail investors in North Texas and surrounding areas. Jennifer is recognized as a leading investment properties expert. Her areas of expertise are in understanding the capital markets, knowing and accessing private capital investors, and underwriting and developing marketing strategies for investment properties in North Texas. She has represented numerous investors in the disposition of their shopping centers, and marketed over three billion dollars in total transaction valuation.

Ms. Pierson began her real estate career working at a firm in Phoenix while obtaining her degree from Arizona State University. Ms. Pierson was named Rookie of the Year her first year at CBRE, and has been a Top 20 Producer in Dallas/Fort Worth virtually every year after that. She has also been ranked as a Top 200 Producer nationally, and is a member of the Colbert Coldwell Circle—an honor reserved for the top one percent of sales professionals at CBRE.

After fifteen successful years as an investment sales professional, Ms. Pierson was asked to lead the United States Private Capital investment group. She successfully co-lead that group for three years, exceeding performance expectations in both recruiting and revenue growth, while continuing to be a top performer in her investment properties brokerage business. In 2013, she made the decision to step out of management and devote one-hundred percent of her time to her own investment sales team.

Website: cbre.us/o/dallas/people/jennifer-pierson/Pages/overview.aspx

Chapter 9

The View from the Sales Floor: A Retail Real Estate Tutorial
by Valerie Richardson

A 1926 *Chicago Tribune* real estate classified ad is credited with first publishing the popular adage that the three most important factors in determining the desirability of a property are "location, location, location." In implementing a growth strategy for a retail company, nothing could be more accurate. Selecting the most appropriate location to reach a target customer is truly part art and part science. However, the process itself is amazingly similar for all retail concepts—small entrepreneurial independently-owned shops, or billion dollar international multi-tiered brands.

Most people don't really think about the process behind a retailer selecting its store locations.

The "image" of a retail brand is the merchandise (well-stocked, right-priced, and neatly presented product), the marketing (targeted, clear brand messaging and communications), and the people (a well-coached, customer-oriented selling and service team), not the physical location or presentation. The highest opportunity for sales and profitability is when all the brand elements work in concert to meet the needs, form an emotional connection, and resonate with the core customer.

Those of us who work in "corporate real estate" are charged with executing the growth of the brands we represent in order to best serve our highest affinity customer base. We have the responsibility of evaluating market potential, selecting locations which meet the company's site criteria, negotiating acceptable business terms and conditions, and facilitating the development of the store. In most companies, a large portion of an annual capital budget is dedicated to store development; occupancy costs are second only to compensation in most companies' profit and loss statements. Although the liability can be significant, the sales potential that a great store location can offer a business is what retail brands rely on.

Every retail real estate opportunity requires vision from the developer, the broker, and the retailer. In building a shopping center, the developer must create an environment which will meet the needs and expectations of the customer base. In creating a brokerage or service business, it is imperative that the broker be aware of, and provide expertise to meet, the needs of his or her clients. Retailers must not only create a concept that is commercially viable, but also must understand what is relevant to their customer in evolving their products, service, and presentation. Each party in the transaction requires expertise in market, product, and customer knowledge and the ability to develop strong relationships with all the parties.

Every retailer strives to craft an offering so unique that it insulates itself from competition and forms a transcending relationship with its core customers. A company's mission will act as a guide for combining its culture, capabilities, and competitive differentiation to establish its place in the retail market. As customers become more time-starved and discerning, the strategic vision of the leadership team helps determine the positioning of the concept relative to the target customer, the product offering, the pricing policy, and the service offering. The product selection is created to resonate with the target customer and to insulate the retailer from competition. The marketing message communicates the brand offering to the customer through multiple channels, developing an on-going relationship through consistent communication. Retailers compose their service strategy to align with their brand position, pricing model, and customer expectation. The most successful retailers constantly evaluate their execution through a series of metrics measuring sales, productivity, and profitability factors to ensure optimal performance. To do so, brand consistency must exist in all areas of the business—product integrity, marketing messages, customer service offerings, even the music played in the store—every aspect of execution is intended to resonate with the target customer.

Retail real estate is, in fact, the physical representation of the brand; in order to best support the brand presentation of the product and services, the location and store design are most successfully executed with both the brand image and the core customer in mind.

Most Retail Real Estate Professionals follow a similar process to determine their store location decisions. Those elements include:

- Corporate Growth Strategies

- Market Analysis and Site Evaluation

- Sales Forecasting and Financial Analysis

- Real Estate Committee Approval

- Lease Negotiation and Store Design

- Construction and Turnover

- Grand Opening

A new store expansion plan is an integral part of a company's overall growth strategy. A retailer's growth comes from the increase of existing store sales, the launch of new merchandising or marketing initiatives, acquisitions, improved selling efficiencies, and an increase in its store base. Short- and long-term objectives are defined and modified to reflect a change in market conditions, competitive influences, customer demand, and resource (both human and capital) availability. New store counts make up the majority of a company's annual capital expenditures, usually allocated as a percentage of sales. Many companies identify "target markets" many years in advance in order to perform the necessary market evaluation.

Individual markets are evaluated for store growth potential. Markets are assessed to determine the appropriate number of stores needed to gain the correct market coverage. The goal is to balance the store coverage for the maximum profitability, brand recognition, and market productivity. The Primary Trade Areas (usually the geographic area in which up to seventy percent of customers and/or purchased sales originate) of each store can be mapped collectively to insure that minimal cannibalization (sales transfer) occurs between stores. Within any geographic area, retailers will utilize multiple objective and subjective site analysis tools to perform a market analysis, including identifying the most dense areas of their core customers, and formulating market coverage strategies.

Depending on the global growth plans, a retailer may take a highly targeted approach to a market—focusing on a single high impact site in the market (think Tiffany's)—or implement a densely stored market coverage (Starbuck's). Coverage strategies are based on the customer appeal to the brand, drive-time tolerance, and product demand. Customers will tend to buy more coffee than diamond bracelets.

Once the market strategy is determined, specific site evaluation and prioritization can be implemented. Each potential site is evaluated first by core customer density, site accessibility, and trade area extent. Retail co-tenancy is critical to presenting a consistent brand message and to attract similar customer profiles to the shopping center. The suitable execution of street visibility, site access, convenient adequate parking, and compelling common areas cannot be underestimated during the evaluation process. In terms of brand execution, the marketing impact, operational coverage, and distribution efficiency delivered by the site act in concert to create the best shopping environment for the target customer. Within larger markets, several site opportunities can be considered while smaller markets may only have one suitable store location that best serves the core customer base. The appropriate store deployment creates a "patchwork quilt" of market coverage that builds brand awareness and supports the most profitable store productivity possible.

As sites are prioritized, retailers will conduct a sales forecasting analysis to determine the sales potential of the prospective location. Some retailers use in-house research departments who have created brand specific models to evaluate a site. Others partner with a third-party analytics firm to develop similar models. Customer data is used to determine the following:

1. The core customer profile (the types of households—sorted by demographics, psychographics, and purchase behavior—with the highest affinity for the retailer's offering).

2. The trade area extent (the average distance that customers are willing to drive to shop).
3. Typical market penetration (what percentage of the population shops, and what do they spend, on average, in a year?).

These metrics provide the input for sales regression, distance decay (sales penetration decreases with distance), and analog models that forecast the sales opportunity that exists in the targeted geographic area.

This forecast forms the basis of the economic negotiations between the retailer and the property owner. Once the sales volume is determined, a retail proforma can be produced. The proforma—an estimate of the future store's profitability—takes all the store expenses into account. Store payroll, occupancy, marketing, supply, and transportation expenses are calculated based on historical trends and known market conditions. If the potential store's profits meet the company target rates for return on investment and operating income, the financial analysis is complete and the transaction can move forward to the next phase of negotiation.

Side note: Occupancy costs are measured as a percentage of the store's sales. The goal on the retailer side is to get that percentage as low as possible; not surprisingly, the landlord wants the opposite. In general, it comes down to which party has the most leverage. In a "buyer's market," the tenant has a better opportunity to negotiate lower rent rates. In high potential markets, where real estate opportunity is scarce, the property owner holds the cards. The parties will negotiate to achieve acceptable economic terms for each side.

As the negotiations proceed, the deal structure is determined. A "gross" lease is a commercial lease where all of the expenses—real estate taxes, insurance, and common area maintenance—are included in one "flat" rate. The property owner bears the risk of increasing costs of the extra charges. In shopping center leases, many agreements are structured as a "triple net" lease, where the extra charges are "netted" out of the rent payment. The tenant will pay their prorata (proportionate) share of the property's expenses, including increases over time in addition to the negotiated rent payment.

If an acceptable return can be achieved through the sales projection and occupancy costs, the retailer will enter into a Letter of Intent negotiation with the property owner. The business terms and conditions are spelled out in detail so that both parties are aware of the financial and legal obligations. The agreement forms the foundation of the final Lease Agreement, which will bind both parties to the terms and conditions of the deal.

In a company conference room, a number of executives gather to focus on a common goal. Each brings a different point of view—the Chairman, President, Chief Merchandising Officer, and CFO—the senior executives responsible for Operations, Store Planning, Development, Market Analysis, and Real Estate. Their collective expertise and perspective is critical to making the best decisions regarding expanding the brand reach of their retail company. This is the Real Estate Committee . . . where each retail store location is discussed, approved, or dismissed. The process is played over and over again through the retail community. Whether the retailer is a small, privately held company with only a few stores, or one of the one-hundred plus publicly-traded retail companies that generate well over a billion dollars in annual sales—the methodology of finding, approving, and developing stores is amazingly similar. All the market analysis, site identification, and preliminary negotiations culminate in the presentation to the Committee.

The real estate package contains all the information specific to the market and the location. Maps and aerials show the proximity to existing stores and orient the Committee to the proposed store location. Customer density, demographic, and segmentation data compares the new site to historical metrics. Site plans demonstrate the accessibility of the site and configuration of the shopping center. Proposed store layouts and elevations answer questions of operational and merchandising efficiency and brand presence. Finally, the projected sales and store proforma indicate the potential profitability and return on investment generated by the location. These materials are reviewed and discussed by the retail team. Questions asked and answered help the Committee determine whether the site appropriately represents the brand, adequately addresses the market potential, and offers the requisite project returns.

Once a site is approved, the retailer will begin the lease document negotiation process with the property owner while proceeding with the development of store design and construction drawings. Negotiations can proceed quickly or drag out for months, depending on both parties willingness to compromise on the details of specific deal points. Typically, both parties are represented either by in-house or third party counsel, although the original "deal makers" are intimately involved in the negotiations. The lease document will outline the responsibilities of each party in accordance with the terms of the letter of intent. The property is described and the length of term—with specific beginning and ending dates, and the availability of any options to extend the lease—are incorporated into the document. Both landlord and tenant roles and rights are spelled out relating to rent payments, sales reporting, construction responsibilities, future assignment rights, and obligations in event of damage or casualty. The tenant's rights to protection for its ability to operate the store as intended, and the landlord's remedies in the event of a default are all specifically defined. Exhibits outlining the site plan, construction responsibilities, signage, and elevations are prepared to reflect the intent of the document. The lease is a legal and binding contract between the parties and will be referred to on multiple occasions throughout the tenancy.

Store design drawings are usually developed concurrently with the lease negotiation. Tenants conduct site due diligence to determine the existing conditions, local building codes, and the property owner's rules and regulations for development. Presentation of the retail brand is critical to creating an impact on potential customers, so the space elevation or façade—with brand-appropriate, clearly visible signage—is carefully considered. Incorporating key branding elements in the store layout—merchandise presentation, cash-wrap placement, and interior graphics—all factor into the store plans. Allocating the space between the retail selling square footage, and the back-of-house functions of stockrooms and staff offices, becomes a critical aspect of setting up the store for operational success, and will vary widely based on the retailer's needs.

Once drawings are complete and approved by the retailer's team, the plans are submitted to the landlord and the applicable municipality for their review and consent. It is not unusual for the city review process to take several weeks before comments are received. All external review comments will be incorporated into the construction drawings, which are re-filed so a building permit can be issued. In some deal structures, the landlord submits the plans, receives the permits, and manages the construction process. In other agreements, the tenant is responsible for the same tasks.

The construction process could include land development aspects—creating the access points, parking area, hardscape, and landscaping—as well as building shell and interior construction, converting a second generation space to a new retail use with exterior and interior elements, or an interior build-out only. Again, either the landlord or tenant will perform all or portions of the development, depending on the agreed-upon terms. In retail nomenclature, a "build-to-suit," sometimes referred to as "design-build" lease, commits the property owner to construct a building which meets the requirements of a specific tenant.

In a "turn-key" deal structure, the landlord usually owns a building that is then converted to meet the tenant's needs and delivered ready for occupancy. In some instances, a retailer will agree to take a space in "as is" condition where the space is offered in its existing condition, with no work conducted by the landlord. The tenant will evaluate the capital investment required versus the proposed occupancy costs to determine whether the project meets its investment criteria under these conditions.

Once construction is complete, typically known as the "turn-over" period, the tenant will accept the premises and install the fixtures, furniture, and equipment required for the retailer to commence its operations. Typically, the tenant will control this phase of the pre-opening process because it involves "tradedress" or brand-supporting displays, graphics, and merchandising, as well as proprietary operational elements. The construction and store set-up process can vary widely from retailer to retailer. Some small specialty stores can be constructed in six week with store openings two weeks later. Other retail stores can take up to a year to develop, given the complexity of their building, improvements, and fixture set-up.

Both the retailer and the developer need to have a thorough understanding of the requirements and the expectations of the other party. Retailers will schedule grand opening events far in advance to maximize the marketing and market awareness opportunities. Efficient project management and good communication will allow both the retailer and developer to optimize the success of the store opening.

Once the store is in the hands of the operations group, the real work begins. Delivering on the brand's promise day-after-day to consistently exceed the customer's expectations allows the company to maximize the productivity and profitability of a new store location. Fulfilling the value proposition with the mission, strategy, messaging, selection, metrics, and service takes the collaboration and commitment of the entire retail team. The process of securing store locations and contributing to the company's growth is both a privilege and an opportunity to "become" a part of the brand.

About Val Richardson

Over her thirty-year retail real estate career, Val Richardson has had the opportunity to work for extraordinary companies— Trammell Crow Company, Barnes & Noble, Ann Taylor, and The Container Store. Her journey through the retail real estate industry has reinforced multiple life lessons, including the value of relationships, the strategic advantage of market knowledge, the need to constantly reevaluate product offerings, the gratification of exceeding the expectations of customers, and the power of working with a team of highly-motivated individuals believing in the same dream. She believes the opportunity to contribute to the growth of a brand is a privilege, creating the foundation to nurture lifelong relationships and inspire far-reaching potential.

Val serves as a Trustee for the International Council of Shopping Centers and its Retail Advisory Board. She is on the Board of Directors of the ICSC Foundation, serving as Chairman of the Scholarship Committee. She is also on the Board of Trustees of Baylor Regional Medical Center at Plano, where she chairs the Quality Committee. Best of all, she's a Grandma.

LinkedIn: LinkedIn.com/pub/valerie-richardson/9/7a6/936

Chapter 10

Keep Your Clothes On and Be Prepared
by Alice Seale

First things first . . . you're wondering about the chapter title, *"Keep Your Clothes On and Be Prepared,"* right? Early in my career, I had a meeting in an office building, next door to another office building which was under construction. I drove into the parking lot (singing my heart out to Tina Turner on the radio), parked, and got out of the car. While walking toward the building, I felt a breeze on my legs. I looked down, and my wrap skirt was ten feet behind me on the ground. Very casually, I retraced my steps, picked up my skirt, and put it back on. Of course I was incredibly embarrassed, but kept my "Graceful Ole Miss Girl" face on—even while the construction workers were laughing and pointing at me. I kept my clothes on—even though in this case it meant putting them back.

Before I started my career in commercial real estate, I worked in sales for a Fortune 100 company. Once, when I was asked about my interest in management, I responded that I was more interested in a discussion on I how I could reach my financial goals. (This same company also asked me to report to Human Resources, where I was told not to wear my cowboy boots with a suit.)

I decided to leave corporate America to pursue career opportunities that held greater potential for reaching my financial goals. In thinking about what I would do next, I recalled a situation several years prior that started with meeting a gentleman at an evening event. After the event, in the parking garage, I noticed that my car had a flat tire. This man had been walking behind me to the parking garage and I asked if he could help me; he graciously did so, then gave me his business card.

When I started my informational interviewing—with an eye toward a career move into commercial real estate—I dug out his card: Hank Dickerson of Hank Dickerson Real Estate. I called him and refreshed his memory of how we had met; he remembered the occasion and agreed to a meeting. As luck would have it, Hank Dickerson's company was starting a retail division. He determined that with my business background, retail leasing would be a great place for me to learn the business. I have always been grateful for the opportunity and what I learned under his excellent leadership.

I believe that commercial real estate is a great career for women. As women, regardless of marital or family status, we have different roles over our lifetimes that require different, and often shifting, levels of responsibility. Commercial real estate is a field that can provide flexibility to juggle your career and family and still achieve financial rewards. In the real estate brokerage segment of real estate, your income potential depends upon you, which eliminates most income disparities between men and women in this career field. This is what attracted me to the industry: unlimited income potential.

In retail real estate, you have an opportunity to work for brokerage companies, developers, or retailers. I have been involved in each industry segment and have learned and grown professionally from each. However, commercial real estate is not a career for the weak-hearted. You have to be your own best mentor, learn to ask for support from others, and have a bigger vision of the world. You must welcome a challenge, relish competition, and have a strong desire to win. I wake up every morning with a positive attitude, believing that I can make a difference in my world, and that the next call I make could financially change my life and the lives of others.

Now, for the second part of this chapter's title: "*Be Prepared.*" Knowledge is very powerful and preparation is essential to compete and win. In this industry, you're on a continual learning curve because of the changing dynamics of retailers expanding, closing stores, and right-sizing their space requirements. The economy is also a factor as it relates to consumer spending and job growth.

I have benefited from market knowledge gained by traveling to major cities to find locations for retailers. Travel exposes you to many different retailers and restaurants, provides the opportunity to see a wide variety of retail shopping centers in other cities, and gives you perspective. It also generates new ideas that you can use in conversations with developers and retail tenants—everyone welcomes new ideas.

I am challenged to become quickly familiar with markets, and prepare for my trips via reviews from publications and my network. Before each trip, I find at least one thing of particular interest to me. An example is Carla's Shoes in Macon, Georgia, which I read about in a magazine. Carla is Otis Redding's daughter, and has the most incredible taste in shoes. (I still have my pony-print pumps that I purchased at Carla's.) I told everyone, "*If you're going to Macon, be sure to visit Carla's Shoes.*" Unfortunately, the last person to whom I made this recommendation subsequently told me that Carla's Shoes is no longer in business.

Lack of preparation can also come back to bite you. For example, one day I was touring a site with a retailer, in a market I had driven hundreds of times. But this day I decided to divert to another area rather than previewing this specific market by myself. The deal didn't happen because the retailer sold one-hundred dollar jeans and the site was in a low-income area—something I would have known had I prepared by previewing that site.

Preparation also includes writing emails, letters, and market presentations. Read and reread, then reread again. I also ask someone else to review my work. Whether sending a letter or proposal by email or overnight mail, think about the total presentation. Visual presentation is important because you want your information not only to reach the intended recipient, but also to make a positive impact. I use a good quality, high-rag-content paper, as well as a high-quality folder for the entire presentation—the goal is a folder the recipient will re-use, and in the process remember where it came from. Some of my favorite folders are mesh with zippers, as well as colorful portfolios—or even a box used as a "folder." I am constantly looking for new ideas at art stores, The Container Store, and paper outlets. My opinion is that you have a greater opportunity for a landlord or tenant to remember you, when initiative and creativity are used.

My dream job came via a referral from someone with whom I worked on the sale of a pad site to Carl's Jr. She represented the landlord and I represented Carl's Jr. as they were expanding into the Dallas market from California, several years ago. They were having a difficult time with the retention of real estate managers; we went through three real estate managers. We did not complete our transaction; a corporate decision was made to put expansion on hold. While we were going through personnel changes, we were building rapport and developing a friendship by the constant communication. We later went to work for different companies, but continually kept in touch with each other. She landed at ING Clarion in leasing the West Coast properties. It is through this relationship that when a leasing position became available, she recommended me. It became my dream job. ING Clarion Inc., which is headquartered in New York City, had a Dallas regional office. I was hired to lease a high-end property in Naples, Florida. I traveled extensively to meet with retailers and review high-end shopping centers all over the country. One September, ING Clarion leasing and management employees gathered at a Boston-area golf resort and conference center for a company seminar. One of the afternoon events was a round of golf at the International Golf Course, with the longest yardage in the U.S. As a beginning golfer, I had played only a couple times prior to playing in this event. And what a surprise—at that evening's banquet, I won a new club for having the longest drive and shortest distance to the hole!

My most personally rewarding career experience was working on a ground-up development in Edinburgh, along the Texas/Mexico border. This development created new jobs and tax revenue for the city. The jobs were with national retailers and provided career advancement opportunities and corporate benefits. The development also occurred at a time when major anchor tenants were seriously considering locating in nontraditional malls, so the development was of potential interest to other anchors and concepts from across the country—and I called them all. Even when they were not interested, they all listened because of the high and increasing level of retail sales to Mexican Nationals. This experience allowed to me to learn the shopping patterns of another culture of people who lived in Texas or traveled to Texas. And I was able to share with my peers my knowledge of the Hispanic community, a hot topic of every International Council of Shopping Centers (ICSC) meeting during this time.

It's also important for women to support one another. As an example, during my tenure as program chairman of Texas ICSC, I was asked to organize regional meetings in major cities along the Texas border. During one of our pre-event planning conference calls, one of the committee members was adamant about an idea for the event that would benefit his company. Although I explained that his suggestion was against protocol for an ICSC meeting, it was quite obvious that this member was not willing to listen to me or accept my comments. Very calmly, a female committee member said, *"I agree with Alice,"* and the obstinate member backed down. I have maintained my relationship with this woman by having dinner with her at state and national ICSC events. Recently, when I needed a "tutorial" on multi-family and senior living developments, she provided information that was essential, relative to the development I was representing. Relationships in our industry are critical in obtaining information to make decisions.

Years ago, I was also inspired by an annual women's luncheon attended by a friend of mine and hosted by Kathryn Hall, former U.S. Ambassador to Austria. Her stories about that luncheon led to my vision for a real estate industry luncheon which would include meaningful networking. I collaborated with two female real estate colleagues in implementing my vision and executing the event. I wanted it to be brief (ninety minutes total of networking) and brilliant (including forty-five minutes of dialogue with a panel of leading national retailers). The event also required me to speak publicly. I prepared thoroughly by writing a script, then rehearsing and rehearsing--public speaking improves with practice. The first luncheon was hugely successful, and it has become an annual December event.

Starting each February, I send letters to a list of potential luncheon panelists, and then I follow up by phone. This has proven to be a great way to build my industry network as I build rapport. Panelists have represented the following companies:

- Barnes & Noble, Inc.
- Darden Restaurants, Inc.
- Footlocker, Inc.
- JC Penney Company Inc.
- Limited Brands, Inc.
- Macy's, Inc.
- Neiman Marcus Group
- Retail Brands Alliance- Brooks Brothers
- Romano and Associates
- Starwood Hotels & Resorts Worldwide
- The Container Store, Inc.
- The Gap, Inc.
- The Gypsy Wagon
- Tiffany & Co
- Tuesday Morning, Inc.
- Zale Corp

The luncheon—my way of giving back to our industry and helping other women—has been a resounding success on many fronts. Commercial real estate attendees have met retailer representatives and subsequently conducted business with them, networked and landed new positions, and maintained and enhanced industry friendships. Although producing this luncheon does require a lot of thought and energy, being successful in *anything* will always require a lot of thought and energy.

My career in commercial real estate continues to give me opportunities to create jobs with my leasing abilities, and to solve problems of landlords with my creative thinking. Although the financial rewards have followed, the most unexpected and valuable rewards are the relationships that I have built and cherish.

"Myself"
by Edgar A. Guest

I have to live with myself, and so
I want to be fit for myself to know.
I want to be able as days go by,
Always to look myself straight in the eye.
I don't want to stand with the setting sun,
And hate myself for the things I've done.
I never can hide myself from me:
I see what others may never see.
I know what others may never know.
I never can fool myself, and so
Whatever happens, I want to be
Self-respecting and conscience-free.

This poem was given to me by a dear friend and is framed on my desk.

About Alice Seale

Alice Seale is principal of Seale Realty Advisors, a firm dedicated to providing real estate, project leasing, and development strategy to both retailers and shopping center developers across the country. Her clients have included JCPenney, Academy Sports + Outdoors, Lane Bryant, Anna's Linens, Hancock Fabrics, Foot Locker, Stein Mart, Zale Corp, Erwin Distributing and Tuesday Morning. Seale founded Seale Realty Advisors in 2009, after a long and successful real estate career with companies including ING Clarion Realty Services, Trammell Crow, First Hartford Realty, and Blockbuster Video. She began her career with Eastman Kodak after earning her B.S. degree from the University of Mississippi.

Seale was instrumental in both the conceptual development and leasing of an open-air specialty retail hybrid center along the Texas- Mexico border, and has managed development and leasing for retailers located in specialty retail centers and in regional community centers. She has also managed real estate franchise transactions. Seale has chaired the program planning committee for the International Council of Shopping Centers and asked to moderate retail panels at regional events. She is also founding chair of Smart Talk Smart Women, an annual luncheon and networking event for executives in retail commercial real estate nationwide. In addition, she is a frequent public speaker for real estate breakout sessions at trade shows.

Seale, a dedicated community volunteer, currently serves as a volunteer for Meals on Wheels. Her additional interests include golf, travel and entertaining.

Email: aseale@sealerealtyadvisors.com
Website: SealeRealtyAdvisors.com

Chapter 11

Don't Swerve When the Business Gets Swervy!
by Karla Smith

*"Coffee in hand, big girl panties pulled up,
sparkle in my eye, and a smile on my face.
Yep, I'm ready for the day . . . bring it on!"*
-Author Unknown

My professional world is commercial real estate brokerage. I am passionate about brokerage, about people, about being a part of something bigger than myself, and about giving back. I am passionate about the art of negotiation, about persistence with a purpose, about women in the business, and ultimately, about bringing success to clients; creating the right opportunity, at the right time, for the right reason. The challenge is doing these things consistently in an *ever changing* and *inconsistent* industry—*the swerve factor*.

"Inconsistency" for this purpose is broad and difficult to define. By inconsistent I mean many things, too many and too subtle to completely illustrate. Some trade variables are obvious; uncontrollable dynamics of the economy, the impact of technology on retail, capital markets variations, growth, expectations, supply and demand, changing trends, brand consolidations, and so on. These variables fluidly change and yet are all conditions of an industry with its own wild variety of competitiveness, personalities, motivations, self-interests, and greed. In this business things can swerve on you, even more so when the stakes are high. As a result, brokers can find themselves brawling over commissions, defending their position, undeservedly circumvented, and compelled to protect their reputation and livelihood.

I have found that by creating my *own* consistency amongst the inconsistency, I stay relevant, grounded, and productive—similar to closing your eyes on a roller coaster and shutting out the chaos to enjoy the ride. My perspective in the business is predominantly related to tenant representation. More specifically, working with retailers and assisting them in managing the process of new store site selection. Inconsistency is common in many sales and commission based professions. Staying real and unswerving can be a challenge.

Choose the qualities that define you and stick to them— *consistently*! I choose *confidence, sincerity, character, code,* and *soul*.

Choose Confidence

Don't let a male centric business stop you. Women provide incredible, immeasurable talents that are uniquely female. Be confident in that. We have something to bring to the table that no one else does. Find your talent and be confident in it like only you can. One of my talents is what I call, "the art of the deal." For me it includes care, creativity, communication, follow through, and persistence. Practices that are not unique, but when consistently and fervently applied, make me different, and that breeds confidence. I enjoy the art of the business and find assurance in artfully making the unlikely become likely, artfully creating opportunities and solutions that don't otherwise exist. Find what makes YOU confident and embrace it, strengthen it, and be confident in it.

Choose Sincerity

We are naturally drawn to those around us who are genuine, purposefully or not. Sincerity is crucial in an industry that can easily be self-serving and fast paced. Sincerity is being natural and authentic in regards to your work and professional relationships; working towards a common goal with realness. People do business with people they like, but it goes further. Loyalty is earned when there is a genuine concern for others and their goals; helping them to achieve them with sincerity. Accept the challenge to be authentic and sincere.

Choose Character

Make your character known. Of course there is no right or wrong, but it is important to be true to yourself, with actions over words. The younger you are in the business, the more important this can be, and even more so as a female in a male centric business. "Character" webs into a lot of areas of interpretation but the bottom line is this: decide what you will and won't do, will and won't say, and make it your wall. It's not a "lead by example" sort of thing; it's a "this is me," sort of thing. This goes for every woman in the workplace. Let your light shine *and* let your character be known.

One of the best compliments I have ever received was along these lines from a male colleague. He shared that over the years, he observed me in various settings performing confidently and skillfully in a man's world without taking on the traits of a man (his words). He said he appreciated the difference in a female that did not adapt to behaviors he had witnessed some females undertake to compete in a male driven business. After reflecting on his unsolicited credits, I realized it was the perfect complement for a female working to elevate the perception of women in the business, and I am proud to know many other women who deserve the same recognition. Impactful comments!

Women are judged differently than men in the workplace. Fair or not, it is reality. Set your character early, letting those around you know your unspoken standards.

Choose Code

Establish a good work ethic. Easy to do, right? Creating a strong work ethic while being conscientious of your goals and the goals of your clients takes tenacity, especially in a commission-based business.

There is an obvious daily work acumen that we work towards, but for me, code is work ethic *plus* how I make a difference for clients—driving the extra route to prepare for the tour, making the extra phone call to determine the unknown, making an extra effort to find an off-market opportunity, coordinating an improbable meeting, or making an introduction that has nothing to do with your livelihood but could help your client in what they do. It is applying both creativity and care to work ethic for the good of all parties. Set your code above the norm.

Choose Soul

Paint with your soul. For me, brokerage is an art. Each day is what I make of it, each transaction is an opportunity to draw, reflect, and grow—an opportunity to bring people together with success in the making. It is for my livelihood for certain; however, it is also to make a difference to those who have entrusted me to assist them in achieving their goals, to get to know them, and to walk a small part of the journey with them.

It's the passion that drives me to make each connection real and sincere.

There are countless personalities, temperaments, and rationales in this industry. Many questions will arise from spiteful behaviors and misuse of influence, leaving you wondering why people do what they do. These questions are bigger than this passage, but open your eyes to it, and realize it. Don't let the inconsistencies change you or the way you treat others. Be real and let your soul guide you.

Stay Focused

Good people, solid companies, great concepts. There are good consistencies for sure. Nonetheless, many of the consistencies can be questionable with the competitive nature of sales, disparity of loyalty, and the self-serving tendencies of the trade. We don't have control over these things, but we do control ourselves. I do best when I stay focused on what drives consistency and keeps me accountable to myself and to my clients; careful not to swerve. My personal considerations include *service, owning it, communication, client regard, persistence, intuition, mute,* and *follow through.*

Consider Service

Be service driven, not fee driven. Do you treat all your clients the same? Do you determine which phone calls to return based on the probability of making a deal? Do you work harder on deals with a large financial reward? I find that some people do, and it results in vast inconsistency for our industry.

If you are in this industry, you know how small the real estate world really is. Anyone can get a deal done. Anyone can get many deals done, but those who are driven by service and not the fee, should fare significantly better in the end. That means possibly missing out on deals you've worked hard on, and often for a long time—deals you started but couldn't support at the end of the day. Service is being responsive, regardless of the anticipated outcome. It is about being true to your clients and true to yourself. If it doesn't feel right, let your client know. Brokers don't make the final call, but we have a hand in the decision by the persuasion and information we provide. Don't let the fee drive you. We are in a service business after all. Be focused on servicing the client, not focused on the fee.

Consider Owning It

Treat your client's business like it is your own. This compliments a service driven mindset. If you think like your client, direction becomes easier. A deal point or transaction that doesn't make sense to you acting in that role, likely won't make sense to your client. Negotiate as they would, to the best of your ability. If you support something, let it be known. Conversely if you do not, put that on the table as well. Ultimately it is their call, but don't get wedged proceeding on something you have concerns about, without sharing your viewpoint.

If you work to understand a client's needs and decision logic, you will be more effective for them. This will enable you to analyze and negotiate differently on their behalf, taking a vested interest, and not letting obstacles deter you until you are absolutely sure it's time to move on. Ultimately, you will have more satisfaction when you complete the best deal for them, knowing you have done your part in their success, as if it were your own business. Own it and own up to it.

Consider Communication

Just as "location, location, location" is important to real estate, communication is important to your work acumen. Communication is a form of consultation: a discussion aimed at ascertaining opinions or reaching an agreement. Communication creates collaboration: the act of working together with one or more people in order to achieve something. This is really the essence of brokerage. We should all be striving to be consultants in our field; to collaborate to achieve. Lack of communication creates uncertainty and doubt. Make real time communication a habit.

On a long-term communication level, keep your clients top of mind whether they are active or not. Active clients are a given, but reach out and communicate with clients who are not active as well. If you don't, someone else will.

Consider Client Regard

Make your clients look good. Be their eyes and ears in the market. Provide them with the tools and information they need to answer questions as it relates to your role. One of the best values you can provide clients in this business is consistent information. Information related to their category, market intelligence, competitive activity, pertinent news, and things that can empower them and help them get their job done relative to your responsibilities. The more they know, the better they look, and maybe the more they can get done with you. They have big territories, they have big quotas, and they have deadlines and stressful committee meetings. It's striving to keep them apprised, and making things as seamless as possible for them. Approaching client relationships with the idea of making them look good builds confidence and loyalty. Extend their reach to make them look good.

Consider Persistence

Pushy? Insistent? Relentless? Not at all. Persistence is resolve, diligence, and thoroughness. You owe it to your clients. Be careful not to go too far, but doing too little can be worse. Along the same lines as, where there is a will, there is a way, don't drop the ball too early on something that is important to your client. We've all heard *"No"* on the other end of the line. The challenge is to understand when there is reason to persevere. We all hit road blocks and have deals die, but they can often be revived through thoughtful persistence. Staying organized will help you stay determined. Make notes and reminders to recall the priorities, and stay on top of them. Persevere for the good of your client.

Consider Intuition

The Radar O'Reilly factor. More than ever, territories are getting bigger, real estate departments are getting smaller, and workloads are increasing. Deals are taking longer and the process is more involved. Your clients have a lot on their plate and you can help them by thinking ahead. Have you ever received a phone call from a client asking for something that you should have called them about first? Give your clients what they need before they need it. This is a form of intuition, as well as enthusiasm and awareness of your client's needs. It takes forethought, but if you focus on what *they* need to achieve, not what you need to achieve, you may determine what they need next—before they do. Be intuitive and prepare your clients to win.

Consider Mute

Listen when your clients are talking, and more importantly, when they are not. They just might be telling you something in the silence—don't miss it.

Often our thoughts fast forward to our next comment or question, before we really understand the issue at hand. Be aware of body language and behaviors that might be telling you something your clients may never verbalize. If you are "on mute," you can hear ways to make their job easier, streamline their needs, and create an opportunity they didn't know they were looking for. I have tested this over time in various situations, and the take away is usually clear: I need to listen to what is *not* being said, or to what rests quietly in the background of a passing comment. Muting preconceived ideas to hear what the client is saying, directly or indirectly, will make you a better broker. Put yourself on mute and take note.

Consider Follow Through

Follow through seems to be overlooked or often disregarded. I believe it is a significant piece of the process, and closes the loop on many of the qualities highlighted in this passage. Have the mindset to service your client, be keen to their needs, and follow through with delivery. Whatever the delivery is—communicating with a particular party, providing information, gathering materials, setting a meeting, etc.—do what you say, and say what you do. Your client may be waiting on a piece of information from you before they can proceed. Just as time kills deals, follow through should be relevant and timely. Be conscious of timely follow through.

A Few More Thoughts

I recently attended a broker conference, and amid all the information, one thing that resonated was a reference to making a difference. The reference was to John Maxwell and his ideology, "*I want to make a difference, with people who want to make a difference, doing something that makes a difference.*" Not new words or phraseology but, *wow*—they were magical for some reason. They relate to any industry, group, or cause. For me it hit home and defines what I am trying to do in the workplace—for myself and for those I encounter. That's it, make a difference . . . one day at a time.

While we all have professional nuances and obstacles to overcome, some are simpler than others. My intent in this passage is to inspire and inform. My insights are given as considerations for those entering the business, or as simple thoughts for those of us who are already in it.

As a clarification, I am not a fan of the term "broker." Although by definition it applies, there is an implication in the word that is not a good fit and does not capture the spirit of what we do. We are more like *agents* for our clients, or "*negotiator, fact-finding, service, knowledge, social, planner, bring it on,*" kind of people. That's why I like being a broker. It is a people business; challenging and exciting, entrepreneurial and bold, refreshing and dynamic, all at the same time. It's good to be in this business *and* be consistent, uncommon, and empowered. I am excited about the business. I am excited about more and more women in the business, excited about trying to make a difference, and about continuing my journey for consistency amongst inconsistency.

For young women entering the business, I encourage you to first establish yourself as a person in the industry while you build on your professional identity. Know that it will take time.

There will be many choices and considerations in front of you each day, like the ones mentioned here. Consciously choose your direction, and stay steady in your choices. Stay real and consistent. Don't swerve when things swerve around you. The rest will fix itself.

"We become what we want to be by consistently being what we want to become each day." -Richard G. Scott

About Karla Smith

Karla Smith manages site selection for national retailers, such as Target and Cabela's in Texas; and Sprouts Farmers Market, Pacific Dental, and United Health Group in Dallas/Ft Worth. In 2009, 2010, 2013, and 2014, Karla was named one of the "best commercial real estate brokers in Dallas" by D CEO and has received multiple UCR Top Ten Awards. She is a Partner at UCR and is involved in ICSC, CREW, and serves on the NTCAR Board of Directors and as Retail Committee Chair. Karla is a founding member of Deals in Heels, a local group of women in retail real estate that encourages the empowerment and collaboration of women in the industry.

Website: ucr.com/people/karla-smith

Chapter 12

Not Your Typical Architect:
Get Your Boots On!
by Karin E. Sumrall

Since I was a child, I noticed my surroundings and could image how much better they might look if I changed them. I moved all the furniture around in my room, created elaborate Barbie houses, and started drawing floor plans. I was destined to be an architect! What is surprising today is that the passion I had early on in my life to design buildings and interiors has evolved into the creativity talent for solving complex problems, working with city jurisdictions and tenants, and leading successful teams in development. Being a licensed architect set the groundwork for my success today.

When I chose my degree, my father told me my buildings would fall down. I had not been the best math student, so I understood his concern. I don't know if he meant to encourage me, but he did, and I was up for the challenge. Before I chose a college, he advised me to interview as many people as possible at architectural firms, find out where they went to school, learn their job roles as they have risen through their career, and obtain their best advice for someone entering the field.

Every summer during college, I worked as an intern for architectural and construction companies to gain work experience to add to my resume, obtain references, and have a better understanding of what size firm and type of work I wanted to do when I graduated. I quickly discovered that large architectural firms would require me to primarily draft technical details within my first few years after graduation. Those firms came off my list. One summer, I worked for a construction company where I wore steel tipped boots and a hard hat, started talking like a sailor (my father wanted a refund on my Catholic education), and learned that many architects really don't know how buildings are built. It was a real eye opener! By the time I returned to college to finish my thesis year, I had a whole new perspective on my profession, and my focus started to change from wanting to design buildings to doing something different with my education. But I didn't know what that was yet.

Bottom line: listening to parents or trusted individuals in your life can steer you in the right direction.

Finding Your Passion

Let's face it. If you don't like going to work every day, it makes your life miserable. When you discover what you really want to do, everything changes. It could happen at the beginning of your career, years into your career, and even by accident, like mine did. One of the first architectural firms I worked for focused solely on restaurant design. I grew up in a family of "foodies," but never imagined this would be my career focus for the next twenty years.

At one of my first jobs, I was fortunate to meet the best mentor of my architectural career. Your mentors will change with each job or role that you are learning. Find someone at every job who can teach you to be the best in your profession, and then learn everything you can from them. After you have mastered your field, remember to give back by becoming a mentor to those starting out in their careers today.

If your degree requires exams to be licensed, complete them as quickly as possible—especially before starting a family. A license, even if not used, adds credibility to your ability to be an expert in your field.

My career path has led me to work for four different types of companies, all of which expanded my knowledge and skill in development: architectural firms focusing on restaurant design; a multi-concept casual dining restaurant company, as concept architect and later director of development; developers, building restaurant and retail property; and director for the restaurant division of an operations company. You will cross paths with prior colleagues many times throughout your career, so make sure you never burn a bridge. You don't know when you might have that person back in your life again.

Each of my jobs further intensified my love of taking on the unique challenge of developing each site or project. Being an architect quickly gained me the respect and credibility of others. Having the ability to debate design issues and focus on the big picture allows me to manage large-scale projects successfully. I finally found want I wanted to do in my career. Now I want to share my knowledge with you.

Bottom line: loving what you do is most important.

Put Your Boots On

While working for the casual dining restaurant company, I gained the knowledge of developing single tenant pad sites and 1.5 acre properties. I furthered my knowledge when I then worked for developers, gaining insight from the landowner's perspective on developing pad sites, and up to one-hundred plus acre projects for large-scale shopping center projects.

The first step in developing any size property requires that you physically walk the entire site. I always bring my civil engineer so we can evaluate budget concerns as we are looking for the following items that we redline on the site plan and photograph:

- Utility Locations—or lack of them

- Topography—which direction and how many feet does the site slope? Will fill be needed?

- Site Access Points

- Signage—drive every street and/or highway to determine site lines, signage placement, and the height for freestanding and building signs. What exists on the abutting properties? Where is the best position for the signage, so that existing buildings or signs do not block it?

- Wetlands/Streams—if you see vegetation running along a path through the property, it typically means there is a stream running through the site that is most likely protected, and cannot be built over easily.

- Site's Prior Use—if the site was a gas station, EPA research will be needed. Or if a gas station is in close proximity to the property, contamination could have flowed onto the site.

- Trees—will the city jurisdiction allow the removal of large species, and if so, do you have to replace with new trees?

- Unique Features—these included things such as rock formations, building foundations, and testing wells.

Every site has issues, even the flat ones! Drive-by evaluations do not work, and here's why. Topography is a major concern with every property because it determines the costs and how to layout your site.

Tall grasses hid the grade changes I found as I was walking a site in Katy, TX (always wear boots on your site visits or at least not heels), causing me to almost fall into a water detention pond. When I got back to the office and asked the real estate manager how the developer was going to address the seven-foot drop-off on the side of the property, they said that had no idea there was a grade change on the site.

Every site has unique features and it is your job to find them. Walking a site in Mansfield, TX that was covered in brush and trees, I came across a fence. Under closer investigation, I found that there were tombstones within the enclosed area, which happened to be in the exact location we had planned the restaurant's patio to face!

Bottom line: do your homework!

Diving Into the Details

Now that you know your site, it's time to find out how to develop it. Today, even the smaller cities are incorporating the big cities' development criteria and processes. Lengthy hearings and upgraded building finishes make it difficult to develop a site quickly and economically. Hiring the best consultants to review and interpret the architectural and civil engineering guidelines and processes is crucial.

I've found the best way to understand the development process is to have one meeting with all the city departments and utility companies. Prior to the meeting, I send them a package, which includes a list of specific site questions and a standard questionnaire my team will be completing during the meeting. In addition, I send the site plan, the signage package for the building and site, and building elevations (if these are available). If you don't have a questionnaire, you need to develop one. It should include the following main categories to help establish the project budget and schedule:

- Utilities—public, private, existing, or need to be extended to the site; costs and timing for electric, gas, water, sewer, phone, and trash

- Planning Department—architectural guidelines, codes, fees, and hearing schedule

- Building/Structural department—codes, schedule, and fees

- Signage—codes and fees

- Environmental Concerns—quality of air, land, and water/wetlands

- Overall Processes—can the project be expedited through the city? Do larger projects warrant the city agreeing to review the plans in a faster process?

The most important thing I have learned is to make sure you gain a full understanding of the city's process during this meeting. Ask questions until you fully understand it. To solidify your understanding, I advise that you verbally outline their process by adding actual hard dates to each step. The fine details of their process will surface (such as second or third review comments, or that the city will take an additional week to wrap up the permit versus the one day you were anticipating).

A partner at a firm where I worked taught me another important lesson. He was a fanatic about legal issues, so he had us log all of our phone calls in a journal, listing the date, project description, the person's name, and a brief description of the main facts of the call. These types of everyday details are crucial to your project and your career. Still to this day, I log my calls. You can't remember everything so write it down. Phone logs are great resources to go back to if you need to remember a conversation and find a contact. I still have the logs from the last ten years in my desk. I never know when I might work in a city again and need to know who the players are!

Bottom line: dive into the details and keep great records.

Building the Crucial Relationships

Your Team

I've found that having the best individuals on your team is crucial. Expect results, but don't ask your team to do anything you wouldn't. If you have an individual who is a "bad egg" take them off the team. Nothing steers the team off course more than one person who doesn't have the same goals and focus. Great leaders seek opinions and listen to their team members. Always provide the encouragement for your team to stretch themselves to new levels while supporting them fully. Celebrate your successes, and analyze your mistakes with your team.

City Official

Establishing a good rapport with the individuals who will ultimately decide how quickly your project obtains approvals is critical. Gain their confidence in your honesty and trustworthiness by doing what you say you are going to do. Never give up your integrity; this will help you negotiate critical project issues with a city. In Rockwall, TX, I was able to work with the planning department and council to eliminate the requirement for four-sided architecture. The back of the proposed buildings abutted an existing truck stop property, which would block the back view of the buildings from the side street. At the hearing, I presented the pictures I took from across the street from every angle clearly showing that the truck stop building and the trucks blocked the view. It was a win-win for all—I saved my company a considerable amount of money on finishes that would never have been appreciated, and worked with the city to add extra items on the prominent building elevations.

City Financial Incentives

At the beginning of the development of any large-scale project, meet with the city economic director and city attorney to determine what financial incentives the city can provide that can greatly assist the overall budget. Each city has different incentive options, such as industrial revenue bonds, public utility rates, infrastructure improvements, tax increment financing, and regulatory exemptions. It is important to learn what is available, as this will greatly assist in determining the overall budget. This can be a long legal process requiring hearings, so it is important to start the process before purchasing the property, or immediately afterward. Cities want new jobs created and tax revenue so find out how they can help make your project a reality.

Land Owners/Sellers/Landlords

If you are the landowner, then you are creating the design criteria for the property. If you are a tenant, then obtaining the landlord's approval will most likely add time and cost to the overall project. Obtain all requirements and schedules to ensure you have the correct process added to the overall project schedule. Some landlords will not allow you to submit to the city without their prior approval, so carefully review this process with your owner contact.

Bottom line: everyone on the project is crucial so set expectations and build strong connections.

Stepping Up to the Podium

Once the project has been submitted and deemed approved to proceed, the city will set the dates for planning, architectural, and city council hearings, if required. Before the hearing, know your "Sacred Cows" (tenant or brand identifiers that are recognized by patrons) and what you are able to concede. You also need to understand the support level by talking to your planner, and if allowed, by attending the pre-hearing meetings with the boards. This will help you prepare for your presentation by addressing any items of concern. The following hearings taught me three different, valuable lessons.

The architectural review board in a city north of Berkley, CA, came in their shorts and Birkenstocks. When I mentioned my tight development schedule, they informed me that they never approved a project after the first presentation. I had walked the site before the meeting and was prepared when asked why we had designed the restaurant to have the restrooms in the front of the building, not taking full advantage of the site views. I quickly mentioned that our building would actually block the view of the existing pawn and gun shop across the street from the remainder of the center. The architectural board member didn't challenge me again for the rest of the night. Issue after issue was brought up as deal killers, to which I quickly countered with design solutions and ultimately, gained their approval that night.

While presenting in San Ramon, CA, I was asked why we didn't have more toilets in our restaurant design. I responded that we met code. I kept quiet while the council members got into an argument that centered around men drinking too much beer, and if men would limit their consumption it would solve the problem. I gained approval that night by sitting back and letting the council duke it out themselves instead of trying to respond to their logic, or lack of it.

In Irving, TX, I was not so lucky. My design team wanted a thirty-five foot tall neon chili pepper to appear slicing through the middle of the building, to make a bold statement for the 25th anniversary of the brand. When I appeared before the city council, two attorneys took the podium against my project. The council went round and round, and eventually told me they could not allow a giant pepper because what if Hooters wanted their image slicing through their building? Before a vote was taken, I asked that the project be tabled, to allow me to work with the opposing council. My lesson that night was that it is best to stop a council voting so it doesn't go on the case record, thereby making it much more difficult to ultimately gain approval in the future. We never built the giant pepper and Hooters didn't build anything either.

Bottom line: be prepared when presenting to city officials, and be willing to negotiate.

The Permit Process

After your project has been approved through the hearing process, it is time to kickoff all of your consultants to complete the construction documents (which can typically take five weeks for a pad site, to multiple months for larger scope projects, depending on the complexity). Sometimes it is worth the risk to kickoff the drawings prior to the hearing process, so you are ready to submit once the project is approved. Many cities will allow construction documents to be submitted prior to the final hearing at your own risk. Permitting is a long and tedious process to obtain approvals from all of the city departments, such as: building, structural, mechanical, electrical, plumbing, civil, health, and those unique to each jurisdiction. Close coordination of your consultants is required, and additional calls and meetings with the city might be required to ensure your project remains on schedule. An expeditor might be needed to push the permit through the city's process more quickly.

Bottom line: be patient and diligent.

Ground Breaking

Once your project is permitted construction can begin. Most cities require a preconstruction meeting with the city officials and utility companies. You will want to discuss the timing of all work they will be performing, and the construction hours allowed. Your solid relationships with the city officials will now roll over to the city inspectors who will assist your construction team. Hopefully, all of your due diligence has paid off and the final phase of the development process will be smooth sailing.

When each project reaches the finish line, take the time to acknowledge your team and the extended team that saw the development to a successful conclusion. Sending gift cards and grand opening invitations to city officials and team members will go a long way to show your appreciation, and pave the road for the next project.

Whether you are literally digging dirt or starting down a new career path, the bottom line is to discover what you are passionate doing. You can fulfill your life-long architectural dream practicing architecture, becoming a developer of retail and restaurant clients, or managing large restaurant rollout operation programs. An architectural degree will allow you to follow an array of careers options. My career path has been a rewarding use of my creative design and problem solving skills. I'm not the typical architect, but I am surely enjoying the path I have chosen!

About Karin Sumrall

Karin Sumrall is the Director of Restaurants for DAVACO, based in Dallas, TX. She has more than twenty years of experience in architecture, project management, site planning, developing one to one-hundred acre sites, retail and restaurant tenant coordination, logistics, and lease negotiations/contract agreements. Karin previously served as a Project Manager at Mays & Company. Prior to that, she was employed as the Director of Development at The Woodmont Company, overseeing new shopping center developments. She held a variety of positions at Brinker International during her ten plus year tenure, including Director of Property Development, leading the planning and execution of new restaurants for Chili's and On The Border. Karin holds a Bachelor of Architecture from Texas Tech University and is a licensed architect in the State of Texas. She is a Dallas native having attended St. Paul the Apostle and Ursuline Academy. She is raising two crazy boys with her husband Darren and resides in Murphy, TX.

LinkedIn: LinkedIn.com/pub/karin-sumrall/33/b53/263

Chapter 13

Some Insights Into
Small Shop Franchise Development
by Jill Szymanski

I think I was lucky . . . I had three people in my life at various points in time that influenced the path I took for my career.

Influencer #1 was my mom, a single mother in the late sixties and seventies. I'm still not sure how she managed everything and achieved what she did, but three of the edicts she gave me that influenced my career were:

1. Get college, and then some.
2. Don't get married until you're thirty.
3. Always be able to take care of yourself.

We discussed lots of other topics and I continually tried to prove her wrong, but the three above were pretty much as we say in the real estate world, "non-negotiables." Of course, when I turned thirty-five and still was not married she did throw a few hints that it certainly would be OK now. I set off to college determined to be a dentist, and soon realized that going to my then boyfriend's baseball games on Friday afternoons was a lot more fun than three-hour chemistry labs. Hence the change in majors from Chemistry to Finance. I finished college and went home to Louisiana, and didn't think twice about going to graduate school with my mom, who was finishing up her PhD in Economics. Yes, imagine going to school with your mother, who certainly was a lot smarter than you and had taken some of the same courses you were taking a couple of years before. All in all it was a good experience, and she did introduce me to *Influencer #2.*

Part of my mother's graduate assistantship in college was working in the finance department of the Real Estate Research Institute at LSU, headed up by CF Sirmans. When my mom finished, he offered me the job to work for him. Originally my plan was to go into the investment area of finance, but working for Sirmans exposed me to the real estate area and I was hooked. Looking at a piece of property was a lot more tangible than a stock portfolio. I was also exposed to the local real estate business with the work we did at the institute, and I made some great connections. One day I walked into work, and Sirmans said, *"Hey, would you like to work for Burger King?"* I said, *"Sure!"* He said, *"Well, go home and change. They will be here in an hour to interview you."* I rushed home, showered, changed into my one "interview suit," and drove back to school. The interview went well and two weeks later I was employed at my first corporate real estate job, Junior Asset Management Representative at Burger King Corporation, working with Influencer #3.

Alan Williger ran the real estate department for Burger King in New Orleans. He had also been an attorney at McDonald's— the company that wrote the "bible" for restaurant retail real estate. Alan and I were involved in a large franchisee acquisition, and subsequent rebuild, remodel, or relocate program for the entire southeastern market. I could not have hoped for a better education into franchise and corporate real estate. I got exposed to some of the most complicated and intricate deals I have ever seen in my career, and we pulled off some amazing results with certain restaurants, more than doubling their volume after the lease was renegotiated and the restaurant rebuilt with a drive thru. Alan had vision and insight and made us see a deal through from beginning to end. I still remember the *"How to fold a survey"* lesson.

Fast forward twenty-five years, thirteen jobs, four companies, two entrepreneurial stints, a marriage, a divorce, two amazing kids, two exasperating dogs, and now my own consulting business. I look back at the ride and realize how lucky I was to have these people and quite a few others in my life who have helped me along the way. Which segues to why I want to share these insights with you on franchise real estate development: I have met all types of franchisees along the way and feel fortunate for those experiences. From brand new franchisees who just left the corporate job they held for twenty years, and now have the entrepreneurial "bug," to franchisees with over four-hundred casual dining restaurants (larger than some actual restaurant chains). They all gave me great insights into what motivates them and makes them successful, and hopefully I was able to lend some assistance to them in one form or another in helping them to get a location open.

Why would real estate professionals want to deal with franchisees? Franchisees are entrepreneurs functioning in a system, and the system is there for a reason. Much like if you're traveling down a river in a canoe. The entrepreneur gets out of his canoe and if he's not sure he's in the right spot he might stop on the bank, wander around in the woods, pick up a few items along the way, and eventually make it back to the canoe to continue down the river and reach his destination. The franchisee gets in the canoe with his franchisor; they have a map, directions, and tools. They stay in the canoe, travel down the river, and reach their destination. For any franchised concept there are processes and procedures in place as well as brand awareness. Working with franchisees as a real estate broker affords you the opportunity to help them optimize their site selection process. Their energies need to be directed to building or remodeling the site, marketing, getting ready to open, and running the business. A real estate broker's expertise helps them understand the retail landscape, the hot buttons of particular landlords, and which spaces will work best for their particular concept. They are typically inclined to drive around looking for spots (they think it's fun), and occasionally they find one, but an experienced broker can make the difference in getting the right deal done. Building that trust, knowing your "stuff," communicating the time it takes to do a deal, and timely responding to inquiries are all keys to a long-term relationship with the franchisee and often, with the franchisor and the landlord.

Another thing that distinguishes this type of deal is the other party to the deal, the franchisor. Franchisors will have expectations and requirements particular to every concept, some being highly systematized and others not. I find this is usually based on the size and longevity of the concept. Emerging concepts typically do not have many resources on the development side, so a real estate professional may find herself doing a lot more work in the emerging concepts arena than in a more established one. Established concepts may have certain absolutes that must be included in leases or submitted in site packages for approval in order to move forward with the deal. It is important to understand what those are, how critical they are to getting a deal done, and the impact they have on the business. It's also a good rule of thumb to validate that a particular franchisee has the authority to do the deal, as well as the area in which they are allowed to expand and develop the concept. On the franchisor side there can also be other factors that could impact a deal. The franchisor company may have communicated to Wall Street that it will open one-hundred units in a calendar year. If your deal makes number ninety-nine and its October, realize that getting the deal done before the end of the year will validate your success with the franchisor group—because you're helping the franchisor keep its public promise.

Additionally, design changes in a brand, pending acquisitions, corporate financing—all these and more—can impact an individual deal. A good resource to get about any franchise concept is a copy of the Franchise Disclosure Document. The FDD contains many details about a company, its management, and how the company structures and manages its franchises and franchise relationships. The franchisor is required to provide you a copy after you have your first conversation with a franchisor representative and certainly before you sign any documents with the franchisor. If you want more information before that first conversation, you can usually obtain a copy of the FDD from the state in which the FDD is filed, or you can get it from online companies such as FranData, which maintains a database of FDDs from a variety of franchisors. Staying in tune with what is going on with the franchisor can save a lot of time, money, and frustration, and enable you to be successful.

So what makes this type of deal attractive to a real estate broker? Not much. Just kidding! If you take the time to understand what the concept is, what the drivers are to the business, what makes a location successful for that concept, what economics work, and know how to work through the franchisor's system, real estate development deals with franchisees can pay off in the long-run in several ways.

The franchisee may end up building multiple locations (most likely because the broker found that primo spot that made the franchisee enough money to open a second and third location) and she might already have other franchised retail concepts for which she may ask the broker to help find the right locations. It is not uncommon for a larger franchisee to have four to five other concepts.

Another way these can be lucrative deals to handle involves the relationship developed with the franchisor. By working through a deal and delivering a quality location, the broker has the opportunity to showcase his/her talents in getting the deal done better and quicker and helping the franchisor achieve its stated goals. The franchisor may very likely recommend the broker to other franchisees in its system. Following up, staying on top of the deal status, and handling issues on the buildout are all things that enable the franchisor to meet its annual and long-term objectives. If you are the person who does this for her, why wouldn't she use you for the other franchisees in the area?

Don't forget in this day and age, many people do not stay in the same role very long. People thought my eight year stint at Applebee's was an eternity. Therefore when someone moves, you have another chance to pick up new business. I have a handful of brokers I have known for twenty years. You can lay odds that when I need a broker in St. Louis, Chicago, Dallas, DC, or Atlanta, I know who to call. I also have associates on the corporate side that I network with sometimes on a weekly basis. I use them as a resource as well, and if one of us needs a recommendation or reference for a broker, we have a conversation about who we have used, in what capacity, and how they performed.

In the actual real estate lease negotiation, there are particular items unique to franchise deals to think about and resolve with landlords:

1. Term—with franchise deals there are generally two agreements tied to a location. The lease and the franchise agreement. The lease needs to have enough

term to coincide with the term of franchise agreement and end at the same time. This rule of thumb becomes a little tricky when the commencement date of the lease is tied to the opening day of the business. One resolution would be to have a hard end date for the expiration date of the lease.

2. Address—I can't stress enough how important it is to get an actual, physical address for the location. Franchisors need this to do its internal analysis; construction needs it for vendors; legal for permits and other approvals. It can save the franchisee a lot of time searching, not to mention errors. If the location is in a shopping center, the name of the shopping center helps as well. It is also important to get an actual space plan and shopping center plan attached as exhibits to a lease. These help tremendously in getting a location approved.

3. Guaranty—with smaller and first time franchisees, landlords may typically require some sort of monetary guarantee. Limit guarantees as much as possible. Some options might be to have a guarantee cover one year's rent and the unamortized improvements, the first two year's rent, or just a set amount to be applied towards rent after a specified period of time.

4. Square Footage and Space Plan—It is critical to having this information be as accurate as possible from the outset. Typically, space plans are conceptual and not as-built. It is always a good rule of thumb to physically measure the space and check the dimensions. I have seen some spaces be off by as much as twelve feet and if a franchisee has specific equipment needs, the

discrepancy in square footage can break a deal after a tremendous amount of time and effort has been invested in getting the location approved. Invest in an electronic tape measure. Also it's a good idea to have language in the lease giving the franchisee the right to re-measure the space. Paying rent for an extra three-hundred square feet that isn't there just takes money directly from the franchisee's bottom line.

5. Performance Clauses—these clauses give the franchisee the right to terminate the lease if the franchisee is not performing well financially at the location. There are always those off chances that the awesome location you found just doesn't work out. A performance clause gives both the landlord and the franchisee the flexibility to move on without additional expense or liability. One "sweetening" option might be to agree to the payment of some sort of monies to exit but try and secure something so there is a known amount rather than an open ended obligation.

6. Permitted Use—the broader the better. Especially with emerging concepts, what a franchisee can do and sell in the space today might not be what that concept evolves to in the future. Having a broad permitted use clause allows the franchisee to adapt to a franchisor's changes quickly without having to wait for the landlord to approve or demand additional rent for a change in the permitted use. Remember, the franchise agreement could be as long as twenty years. Who thought twenty years ago McDonalds® would be selling salads or that Taco Bell® would be selling breakfast items?

7. Exclusivity—do you really want to your franchisee to have a direct competitor right next door to them? Typically, lack of exclusivity can impact twenty to sixty percent of the business. Will the franchisee make that much money to afford that sort of sales transfer? The rent a franchisee (or any tenant) pays is based on the location and what the tenant mix is today, in the particular location. If the landlord wants to add competitors in the future, and the landlord won't agree to exclusivity, at the very least the broker should secure some sort of rent concession.

8. Radius Restrictions—I have seen these as broad as any concept the franchisee operates or citing the actual concept. These clauses do have some validity if the lease has percentage rent but typically these clauses should be deleted. Also pay close attention to what the franchise agreement lists as a protected area. A franchisee cannot agree to a radius restriction greater than the protected area in the franchise agreement.

9. Assignment—a franchisee needs to be able to transfer to another franchisee without the landlord's consent. This concept can be negotiated in a variety of ways with emphasis on the financial strength of the assignee. I typically like to use a store test, i.e., "as long as the approved franchisee operates at least X number of units." It's easy to measure and determine while a net worth test requires financial statements and there is no exact, accepted definition of net worth test. Having a very simple assignment required can also be very important for the franchisor which, in the middle of an acquisition doesn't need to delay the closing of its deal

while waiting for a landlord on one location to agree to the assignment of the lease to the franchisor.

10. Relocation—landlords like to have the ability to relocate a concept anywhere in the center and sometimes change the size of the space as well—especially with smaller or less-established concepts . Imagine that a franchisee secures a great spot right at the entrance of the shopping center with plenty of parking. After a year, the landlord then moves the concept to a larger space in the back corner wedged between two busy restaurants. The franchisee now has no visibility, customers can't easily park, and the franchisee is now paying more rent. If you have to agree to something, make sure any associated costs are covered, rent is decreased or stays the same, all signage is still allowed and the relocation space is comparable with respect to parking, visibility and access, and try and designate where the landlord cannot relocate the concept on a site plan attached as an exhibit to the lease.

11. Signage—more is better. Don't forget additional signage opportunities such as on the pylon of the shopping center or on the back of a building that might be visible to the street or highway. The time to ask is before the lease is signed. Always a good idea to drive the entire shopping center and see if there might be a better location . Finally, remember to negotiate continuing signage if the landlord wants to relocate the space.

12. Lease Addendum—although the franchisor is not a party to the lease most will want the ability to come in and take over if the franchisee defaults under the franchise

agreement or the lease. Many franchisors want the right to operate the location themselves or put another franchisee in place without remaining liable on the lease. Other items may include the franchisor's right to approve any changes to the lease and the right to operate the concept in the event of a default by the franchisee. This is a document that the franchisor may sign in addition to the franchisee and the landlord.

Overall I prefer to outline these items up front in a Letter of Intent. It gets these points out on the table early on and saves the deal from getting bogged down when a lease gets to attorneys. Also the franchisee can make a better economic decision knowing the extent some of these clauses might impact the location and, therefore, the franchisee's bottom line. While getting open is important, being able to stay open profitably for the entire term of the franchise lasts a lot longer. No one knows what will actually happen over the entire term of a lease. Building in some flexibility allows franchisees to operate successfully or exit from a deal so they can move on. As the person who represents them you can assist in this process and hopefully reap the benefits both financially and professionally that help you as well.

For those of you contemplating a career in real estate or those who have recently entered the arena, my best advice would be to get in and do the grunt work first and align yourself with industry leaders and knowledge experts. If they ask you to go back and drive a trade area, check maps so retailers are in the correct location, compare Letters of Intent to Leases, do it! Sometimes we don't realize the benefits of the things we have to do until later. There are invaluable lessons to be learned from people in the industry who have seen the life cycles of concepts you can't contemplate coming in. Moreover, you are building credibility and friendships. I have met some lifelong friends along the way and enjoyed or at least learned from every moment.

About Jill Szymanski

Jill Szymanski has spent the past twenty years in corporate and franchise real estate working for large international retail companies and emerging concepts. In between that time she also owned her own flower shop and restaurant. Now as President of SZY Consulting, she helps companies and franchisees find solutions for their retail real estate from individual real estate deals to setting up their departments and implementing analytic models. A bit of a vagabond, Jill currently resides in Dallas, Texas with her two children, one rescued hyper-active Miniature Pinscher and her loyal sidekick a Corgi mix. In her spare times she enjoys watching her son's lacrosse games coaching her daughter's team and scuba diving when she can get away.

LinkedIn: LinkedIn.com/in/jillszymanski

Chapter 14

How to Succeed as a Commercial Real Estate Lawyer ~~Without Even Trying~~ by Trying Really Hard
by Harriet Tabb

I arrived in Dallas on October 6, 1985 with my shiny new law degree from Stanford Law School and an eagerness to work in commercial real estate, hoping to have an interesting and remunerative career. I have gotten everything I could have hoped for, and then some, but it didn't always happen the way I expected.

EARLY CAREER ADVICE (FIRST TWO YEARS)

The Best Way to Learn is to Do

I often say the best thing that can happen to a new lawyer is to be insanely busy for at least a year, preferably two. So my first piece of advice is that you take on every possible piece of work and try to do as much as possible by yourself. You'll probably screw some things up (and if you do—seek help then), but even your screw ups will be instructive. At the end of my first year, I represented a lender who was selling some of its foreclosed property and financing that sale. Since I didn't have a secretary who would do my work (a common problem at the time), I had to use word processing. We went through a lot of drafts and at some point word processing began making the changes to a much earlier draft, so that all intervening changes were lost. I wasn't checking to make sure that changes I had already seen were still there and eventually, these wrong documents were signed. After the executed documents came back from the title company, I was flipping through and, in a blood-chilling moment, noticed the errors. I had to call the client and tell them, clean it up for free (thankfully, the borrower cooperated, but not very graciously), and watch nervously several years later when it was again foreclosed upon and the guarantor sued. Thankfully, it all held up, but it was excruciating. My first lesson was to always do a final re-read, something I still do today. My second lesson is that every single lawyer has a story like this. Whenever I talk about this mortifying error, other lawyers will start laughing, eager to tell about their first horrible disasters. The exception, obviously, is the lawyer from California who left some zeros off of the proof of claim in Bankruptcy, which couldn't be corrected. That poor associate lost his job and I bet he still doesn't see the humor in the situation.

Learn Something from Every Experience

If something goes really well, figure out why it went so well and apply those lessons to make other projects go well. If something goes poorly (see above), then learn what to do to avoid those problems. Here are the lessons I learned early in my career:

- The best deals meet the core needs of both parties as much as possible. It may seem like a great thing to get everything you want at the expense of the other party, but in the long run, that's not a good basis for a happy relationship (this obviously applies in other contexts as well). I worked on a theater lease in a time in which theaters were going under right and left and the tenant thought they deserved a lot of concessions because they were one of the survivors. My client disagreed and there was a rather vehement "discussion" with both parties declaring they could not work together. The next morning, I was on a flight and sat right behind the tenant's representatives. I was surprised and asked them why they were leaving. They looked upset and said they thought the deal had died. I said, *"Well, it doesn't have to die. Why don't you try again? But remember that a good deal has to be as good as possible for both parties."* They landed, went back, and made the theater deal. That theater is still successful (and I don't get the credit for my intervention, but that's a different story with which most lawyers can sympathize). Obviously, there are sometimes deal points that can be difficult to work through, but it's very common for one side to insist on something as a power play, rather than because they really need it....which brings me to the subject of bullies.

- Bullies are insatiable—stand up to them the first time they try to bully you. You can usually spot bullies very quickly and it's important that you tell your client to stand up to them the very first time they try to bully you. No client should act as if it is desperate when it is merely very eager. There are times when desperation is appropriate, but it's not as often as people act like it is. Once a client has shown its willingness to be bullied, the bullying will never stop. The very worst thing about giving in to bullies, besides the psychological price, is that the final agreement—which is usually in effect for a long time—is so terrible for one side that they simply cannot do what they need to do to make money.

I saw this with a retail developer who wanted to develop a retail district in a downtown area, much to the displeasure of the office building owners. Because there was political pressure on the office building owners to allow this kind of development, they entered into an agreement that ostensibly permitted retail in the first floor of their buildings, but imposed restrictions and conditions that made it impossible to find tenants who would agree to go into the space. The developer accepted it because they thought they had to. I, fortunately, did not have to endure the initial negotiations, with my client being cowed by the bullying. I understand that the lawyer who went through that process left the practice of law soon afterwards and his partners all blamed that transaction. But it was horrible to watch my client try to actually lease the space, a situation that improved only when a less difficult owner bought the buildings and didn't enforce the terms of the agreement.

- Understand the other party with whom you are negotiating. Sometimes, people come together in business deals thinking they share a vision with the other party based more on what they want to be true than what is actually true. I recently worked on a transaction where our client wanted to acquire a development that had been allowed to get run down. They were going to re-develop the project and improve some of the vacant property around it. Unfortunately, the previous owner had entered into a sale/leaseback arrangement and my client was going to have to step into the shoes of the "tenant." I was in charge of reviewing the lease. As I read it, it became obvious that the landlord's only interest was in maximizing income while minimizing investment (the "slumlord approach") and they would never allow for the kinds of upgrades and improvements my client wanted to make. I checked around and the slumlord approach is, in fact, what this company is known for. It ultimately killed the deal midway through the process, but I think my client would not have wasted any time trying to put the deal together if someone had investigated the landlord a bit more.

Figure Out What You Do Well: Try to Do That as Much as Possible

Everyone has their strengths and weaknesses and you aren't doing yourself any favors by telling yourself you do everything well. It's best if you can identify your strengths as quickly as possible because then you will spend more time doing things you do well. Since most people prefer to do things they do well, you'll be happier. In fact, if you are having a hard time identifying what you do well, think about what you like to do. That'll probably be a good clue. I've described my personal analysis below, but I encourage every young lawyer to do the same kind of analysis and then figure out what kind of work plays to their strengths. As for myself, I obviously tried to be good at as much as I could possibly be, but I found pretty quickly that I enjoyed complicated negotiations and drafting the agreements that resulted from those negotiations. I did not enjoy statutory analysis at all (I figured *that* out in law school and that was why I did not become a tax or securities attorney). And I didn't really enjoy knowing the ins and outs of arcane area of the law.

- *No mortgage lending*—that meant I did not enjoy mortgage lending work because the negotiations aren't very important (if you are the lender, it's just variations on saying "no") and the drafting relies on forms you have no ability to update (meaning fix) because they are the lender's etched-in-concrete forms. And, at least in Texas, you have to understand usury, which is the Platonic ideal of "arcane area of the law."

- *Maybe commercial lending*—I liked commercial lending a bit more because I was lending to businesses and so have to obtain liens on all kinds of assets, from real property to accounts receivable to corporate shares. The due diligence was fascinating (except the time I had to read the source lists for a company that made fertilizer; that was memorable, but really gross). But I think what I liked the most was learning about the specific businesses that were borrowing the money. It seemed kind of second-hand to learn about a Borrower's business when I was representing the lender, so I decided to focus on an area where I could learn a lot about my client's business, participate in negotiations, and draft complicated agreements.

- *Retail development and leasing fit the best*—and that's what retail development and leasing have done for me. Many people think a big sale is the most complicated matter a lawyer can work on, but it's not close. I handled a huge sale of a property that made the Wall Street Journal as an important deal, but there was nothing difficult or complicated about it. A sale is over and done with in a very short period of time. A lease, however, is the game plan for a relationship that everyone believes and hopes will last amicably for a very long time. And retail leases have the most complicated game plan because the actions of each party affect the other in so many different ways.

- *Figure out what your weaknesses are and develop compensating behaviors.* Every work habit has a good point and a bad point and you need to figure out what your bad point is and take steps to avoid having it impact your work. If, like me, you work very quickly, then be sure to re-read your documents before they are signed, especially if there are a lot of drafts, a lot of drafters, or a lot of time elapsed from the beginning to the end of negotiations. You might have to discipline yourself to slow down a bit. If you tend to get lost in the forest and wake up to realize you haven't made as much progress as you thought, you might need to always start with an outline. But really, only you can decide what problems you need to address. But you should address them.

ADVANCED CAREER ADVICE

Learn as Much as Possible About the Businesses You Serve

You will be of immensely more help to your clients if you have at least some understanding about how their business works and what matters to them the most. Obviously "making money" is why they are in business in the first place, so what you are really doing is figuring out what makes it possible for them to make money. There is so much that I have learned about retail and mixed-use development, management, ownership, and leasing that it's almost impossible to list all of the items, so I decided to just pick four items that I thought would help to avoid some of the worst mistakes I've seen clients and others make.

1. *200,000 SF Minimum*—I know that a good retail development needs to have at least 200,000 square feet, preferably ground floor, which is why all those tiny little retail areas in apartment complexes that are labeled as "mixed use" are never very successful.

2. *On Site Demand Insufficient*—I have learned it's almost impossible to create all of the demand for retail and restaurants out of the people "on site"—you need more than a captive audience to be successful.

3. *Retailing Front and Back Ideal in Mixed-Use.* I think tenants should have a more open mind about retailing out of the front and the back, because my experience is, they all reject it until they open up and realize that customers are arriving from all directions (often tied to the parking arrangements) and want to retrofit to allow it. This has been a problem in the majority of the mixed-use developments I have worked on

4. *Landlords Need to be Flexible in Programming*—I think developers sometimes become enslaved to their programming of the space, when it would be better to build in some flexibility in case the tenants don't have the same idea of what would be perfect as the developers do. Developers make certain decisions based on their programming that are hard to unmake. It would be better to have built in some flexibility.

Watch What Happens in the Business Community (aka, "The Benefits of Disaster")

I arrived in Dallas at the same time as the S&L crisis and watched the disaster happen in real time. Although it was scary to begin my career in this environment, I learned so much from what happened then, that I don't regret it. One junior developer of a client and I went to lunch and then to visit his latest shopping center, which was completely empty. We just sat in the car and laughed because what else could we do? I often saw deals that had been put together in a slapdash manner during the "go-go" days having to be unwound, where all the glossed-over problems and internal inconsistencies suddenly meant something—and not something good. And I learned the following lessons:

- *Things will never stay in the trajectory they are in now.* Values that are ballooning up will not only slow in their increase, but will almost certainly decrease and it's good to always keep that in mind. The reverse is also true—plummeting values will go up some day. Don't get too giddy or too depressed.

- *No matter how hot a market is, no good comes from ignoring basic investment or underwriting principles.* This truism is proved over and over and over again and, sadly, forgotten just as quickly.

If you read the stories of the Penn Square bank scandal from the early 1980s, the bank raised money by selling "participations" to other bank. The investor banks paid no attention to the underlying loans, few of which were properly underwritten or documented and many of which defaulted.

The investor banks suffered a series of unpleasant surprises. First, the loans they hadn't bothered to investigate were terrible. Even worse, their "quick and easy" documentation gave them a valueless claim against an insolvent bank, rather than an ownership interest in the loans and liens securing them that would have enabled the investor lenders to get some return on their investment.

Many of the loans that led to the S&L crisis of the mid and late eighties involved valuations that were unmoored from the income that the tenants were paying or any tenant ever could be expected to pay except in fairy tales that begin, "once upon a time, property valuations went up and up and up and they never ever came down again."

The same thing happened in the CMBS Market. Cutting the loans into tranches didn't create more value, but it did appear to divorce the investment from the underlying loans, enabling the buyers of the tranches to completely ignore all of the many underwriting problems.

As I was writing this chapter, I was struck by two things. First of all, and not really the point of this book, it's interesting how many of these observations apply to far more than a legal career in the area of retail and mixed-use development. And second of all, I am very lucky that I have done and am able to continue to do, work that I find so interesting.

About Harriet Tabb

Harriet Tabb has worked in the area of retail and mixed-use development for nearly thirty years, earning the reputation of being "tough, but fair." Her clients appreciate that she identifies and solves problems before they arise, beginning with the initial development, where her experience allows her to help landlords avoid common pitfalls, continuing through the lease-up process and on into the mature phase of development, and eventually with the sale of the project.

Website: mcslaw.com/attorneys/harriet-tabb

Chapter 15

Leaving Pieces of My Life Behind
by Liz Trocchio-Smith

There weren't a lot of women when I started in the commercial real estate business. In fact, there were very few.

Over the years, I followed some, led some, and walked beside the others. I didn't realize then how much of an impact I would leave on so many of their lives. Still now, they tell me I make a difference that meeting me somehow changes them, makes them want to be a better person. It's humbling, really. Because it's just me, doing what I do, what I have always done. Yet my journey really has just begun, and I know now I am doing what I was always meant to do: help people, develop leaders, and coach professionals on how to achieve their true value.

So it would probably surprise you to know that I'm the daughter of an alcoholic father, a verbally and physically abusive man who told me every day—several times a day—that I was good for nothing. After hearing it day after day, you begin to believe it. How could I grow into a positive force for others? Because I had an amazingly strong mother, and her love for my siblings and me reinforced we could do and be anything. Plus, I was determined to prove my father wrong! After leaving my father, my mom raised four kids on her own, with no support from my father. She worked two jobs, and put herself through college. I got my toughness and my no nonsense attitude from her! I share this because I feel it is important to understand my background and the resulting self-esteem problems I faced growing up. Why? Because this same issue followed me into the business world. Low self-esteem and low self confidence is at the root of many self-imposed limitations for women in business. So take it from me: don't let low self-esteem stop you! Let it motivate you instead.

One of the first professionals who openly shared with me that I made a difference in his life was a man. It was after I was leaving one office to move to another and he wanted to make sure I knew I had impacted his career, and his life. He gave me a framed picture that still hangs in my office today. The picture is of a funny little character dancing and dropping little bits and pieces into a bag, and the caption beside it reads, *"She left pieces of her life behind her everywhere she went. It's easier to feel the sunlight without them, she said."* It's a precious gift.

And so my journey began.

When I entered college I wanted to be the next Barbara Walters. To get a degree in journalism and follow in Ms. Walter's footsteps, interviewing heads of states and world leaders. I worked putting myself through school, so in 1980 when I was offered a job for a commercial real estate firm in Dallas Texas, when the industry was booming, I knew it would be a great way to earn a living and pay for college. Then, brokers who brought tenants to buildings and leased space were winning Mercedes and Rolexes! And let me tell you, it was the American Dream come true. Everybody and their brother wanted into the business.

But the mid 1980s would bring the commercial real estate bust, and with that a commitment from that same company that I could keep my job if I learned to lease industrial warehouse buildings. A job was a job, and my momma didn't raise a fool. So learn to lease is what I did. Quickly I learned that leasing industrial warehouses in Dallas, Texas in the

August heat was not what I wanted to do forever, but I learned everything I could about it and I began to succeed.

I listened, and I watched, and as I grew in the commercial real estate industry, the idea of becoming the next Barbara Walters would become a distant memory.

Watching my mother raise a family alone and receive her college degree, reminded me that I could do anything, so tough came easy for me. And so did admiring her. I learned a lot from her by watching and listening.

As I continued my journey in commercial real estate, I fell in love with the industry. It was exciting to be part of something so full of energy and challenges, and every morning I woke up to something different. The most important thing then, that still holds true today, is that the commercial real estate industry has one solid foundation that it is based on relationships. There is an old saying, *"It's not what you know, it's who you know."* That saying could not be more truer here than anywhere else. That is the great thing about commercial real estate, and in Dallas, Texas, it is unique. It is a friendly, competitive industry like no other you will find across the country.

I learned that my talent was not in leasing but in people. Leading people. When I was given the opportunity to move from a leasing position to a management position, to manage and lead people, that's when I began to thrive. I was helping people and utilizing talents that came naturally, and people responded naturally. The pieces of the puzzle were coming together.

I spent thirty years in commercial real estate climbing the proverbial corporate ladder and working very hard to make it in a very male dominated world. But I was ok with that. I liked men, and I liked working with men. Still do on both accounts. They didn't threaten me and they didn't intimidate me.

Unfortunately, and quite sadly, it was the women I had to watch out for. Since our number was so limited, I would have expected us to be more than willing to help one another. But that was not the case at all. Women in commercial real estate weren't very friendly to other women and they still aren't at times. I found this very disheartening. But I refused to be one of them. I thought it was petty and silly.

So back in the day, men had their "clubs" and "good ole boys networks" which I of course was not allowed to be a part of. But then finally, in the mid eighties, women in Dallas founded their own "good ole girls club." It was called Commercial Real Estate Women—CREW for short. Founded by women for women, CREW was first and foremost a networking group. Members gathered to help each, to do business together, and to find ways to work together in this commercial real estate industry made up of all the "good ole boys." What a great concept, huh?

It is still going strong today, and is now a national network of approximately 11,000 women across the country and Canada. And yours truly is a Past President of the Dallas Chapter, a Past Outstanding Achievement Award Winner of the Dallas Chapter, and a Past National Board Member. Some of my best friends, who I met in the business and still have today, I met in CREW.

Over the years, I saw more and more organizations such as these form to help women get together and find strength in numbers. Funny thing is, men began to feel left out. Go figure, right!

So women were starting to make a name for themselves in commercial real estate, and personally, I was too. I continued to work hard and was promoted in several areas and jobs within the business. At one point, I was working on the property management and leasing side of the business and was enjoying the challenges and the people I worked with. But when the company I worked for was sold, which happened a lot in those days, the job I was doing was redundant to someone else in the company that bought us. I got laid off. It was the first time I was out of a job, and I was pretty shaken. I was single, had a mortgage, but I dusted off my resume and jumped right back into the job market.

In less than ninety days, I was moving into my new office as President & COO of a regional development, management and brokerage company.

Ok, so it wasn't as easy as it may seem. I had to call a lot of people, and a lot of people I called didn't call me back (as much as I hate to admit it). I went on a lot of interviews for jobs I didn't particularly want to take, but I was patient, (most of the time) and I was confident (again, most of the time) the one job I really wanted would come my way. I knew if I talked to one person they might lead me to another and some other contact might get me in touch with someone else. That's how it had always worked. And it did again this time. The job I really wanted, I got. But it took time, patience and planning.

That was a tough time in my life, and what I remember most is two things. Wondering how I was going to pay my mortgage, and the rejection I felt when I didn't get calls returned to me when I needed it most. So I made two promises to myself. One, I would make sure I had enough money in the bank that if I got laid off again I wouldn't care, and two, I would always take someone's call, or return it, or respond to them somehow, because everyone, everyone, has fifteen minutes to give someone else. I kept both those promises and they still hold true today. I challenge you to do the same. It will make you a better person.

So now I'm what many would term a big dog. Although I am not sure I appreciate the exact word picture this conjures, I understand the analogy. I became President & COO of a company and I made some major decisions every day. That's important because I drove some essential outcomes to my company's bottom line and made a real difference to my employees.

Leading came naturally for me. I had learned from some of the best, and the worst, leaders in the industry. I knew what to do, and most importantly, what not to do. I remember my first week on that job. A young man walked into my office and he said he wasn't going to work for a woman. Well, it just so happened he reported directly to me, and I was a woman, so, I figured we were in a bit of a quandary. I told him I wasn't planning on leaving, so I could only assume he was giving me his resignation. He stuttered a bit and slowly left my office. He must have thought about it for a few days because he came back later that week and he did resign. Seemed his father was in the business and he preferred working for him. I guess I never really understood how he knew that since he never really worked for me, but he made his choice and I wished him well and he left. I don't think we ever missed a beat. I wish no one ill will. Life is all about choices. Remember that.

I spent the next six years making a difference at that company. It was the age of websites and email coming into the business world and we were far from change agents. We were so far behind the eight ball, but I finally convinced them to adopt and embrace email and build a website. It was baby steps, but I helped get them into the twenty-first century. We had a lot of success; I added some fantastic talent and a large amount of business to the portfolio due to relationships I had fostered over the years. Then I received an opportunity that I couldn't refuse. It's the, "life happens when you least expect it," thing. I was very happy doing what I was doing, where I was doing it and who I was doing it for, but the next step in my career had come knocking on the door, and I had to answer it.

So I went from President & COO of a regional firm to a Senior Managing Director of a global firm, and I was truly excited to see what the future had in store. I found it to be a great ride, and it would take me to my next destination. I would spend the next eleven years working for a company where I would truly grow and thrive in. Not just professionally, but personally as well.

It was the dawn of the age of diversity, and women were needed in leadership positions. I was proud and honored to have been sought out for the one I was just hired into. I was looked at as someone who could make a difference for women, not only in the company, but in the industry as well, and I was proud of it. I went from running a local office for the global firm while managing five disciplines, to expanding my responsibilities to leading the central US over those eleven years. I was good for the company and they were good for me.

Throughout my career, I learned that gender wasn't an issue unless you make it an issue. So embrace your own diversity. I worked with some of the smartest peers and senior leaders in the industry and we were making a real difference. I grew very quickly in the company, started a lot of training programs for young up-and-comers, coached and mentored many professionals and developed an internal woman's networking group which the then CEO of the company personally reached out to me and asked for my help to build. It was a tremendous success: 1500 strong globally, of Women Helping Women, and that made me realize that not inside the company, but inside the industry and inside corporate America, women did not help each other enough.

And that all brought me to where I am today. I believe both men and women need to hear my message. Men expect that women will not get along, so they smiled knowingly and waited for the catfight. And women, well, I don't have enough space to talk about why women can't get along in the business world. That's what I do today, I help them. It starts at the beginning with the small thing called "self-esteem" and grows from there. When mentoring a new client, I like to start with the following anecdote:

> *A group of women are at a networking event. A tall, thin, attractive woman walks into the room, confident, dressed sharp and there for the same purpose as everyone else: to network. But her confidence turns everyone else off and they ignore her. They are intimidated by her, threatened by her, and immediately don't like her. Seriously? Ladies, there is business there. She doesn't want your job, she doesn't want your office and I promise you she doesn't want your* **husband***! She has one of her own! She may want to know where you got your fabulous shoes and matching purse, but she wants to do business with you!*

Here are five important facts to remember along with the tips I shared throughout my journey:

1. *Women Helping Women*—check your insecurities and low self esteem at the door! We all have it, and it's ok, but put it away for a while. Women *must* help other women! We have to create a path for our daughters and granddaughters to come after us.

2. *There's No Crying In The Boardroom*—I mean this! Do not cry . . . no matter what! It is a sign of weakness. If you have to cry, do it behind close doors when no one is

watching, and throw whatever you want and scream too, but not in front of anyone!

3. *Your Reputation Is All You Have*—always, always, do the right thing. No matter what.

4. *Pay It Forward*—you have time to help someone else. It's important to them and it's important for you. Just do it.

5. *Appearance*—I always stress that women should dress for the job they want and not the job they have. We always want to look professional. Dress like a CEO. Overdress, don't underdress, but by all means, be dressed! Don't show body parts no one really wants to see in a boardroom; that goes for low cut blouses and skirts too short!

When I left corporate America, I decided to do something different. I wasn't sure what that "something different" was until I began talking to people and learned they were clamoring for sound, well-reasoned career advice. I wanted to give back, to help people, to make a difference. So I got my coaching certification and became an executive business coach. I had to have two paying clients before I could receive my certification, and when I had ten paying clients, I knew I was on to something; the consulting assignments and public speaking engagements came shortly after as a bonus. Now, everything I do I consider a bonus, a gift.

As the writing of this book, I have just been accepted to SMU's (Southern Methodist University's) Cox School of Business Executive MBA Program, because I know how important it is to continue to educate myself and to keep my clients informed of important business decisions they are making. I may not be interviewing heads of states and world leaders, but at the end of the day, I'm "just leaving pieces of my life behind me everywhere I go and basking in the sunlight!"

she left pieces of her life behind her everywhere she went.

It's easier to feel the sunlight without them, she said.

About Liz Trocchio-Smith

The "Liz Factor" blends intuition, deep business experience, and personal success that enables clients to pull themselves out of their comfort zones, find their "aha" moments, and rise to the occasion to get to the next level. Clients trust Liz and say that just working with her makes them want to be better than they are today. Liz Trocchio-Smith brings irresistible energy, an optimistic and encouraging style, and a devotion to creating synergistic relationships that deliver results.

With a successful and visible career in commercial real estate, Liz has been a top executive of such well-respected companies as Cushman & Wakefield, the Woodmont Companies, and Hines. Her accomplishments have led to numerous awards and appointments to both internal and external Boards of Directors. Throughout her career she has coached and mentored high potential professionals who subsequently grew in their careers and established themselves as players in the industry, along with proven leaders continuing to help them grow in their positions of authority and power.

Liz holds a BBS in Business from Dallas Baptist University and is working on her Executive MBA from SMU's (Southern Methodist University) Cox School of Business. She is an Associate Certified Coach (ACC) through the International Coach Federation, the leading global organization for coaches, a Certified Executive Business Coach through the Coach

Training Alliance, and a licensed Texas real estate broker. Liz is a frequent and sought after guest speaker at conferences, workshops, and seminars.

Email: Liz@TrocchioAdvantage.com
Website: TrocchioAdvantage.com
*LinkedIn:*LinkedIn.com/pub/elizabeth-trocchio-smith/35/507/452
Facebook: Facebook.com/TheTrocchioAdvantage

Chapter 16

Landing in Heels:
The Art of Being the Successful Female
Candidate in a Male Dominated Industry
by Lisa Walker

In the world of commercial real estate we are only as good as our last deal but nothing feels better than landing the next one! And when we find ourselves looking for a new role at another company we have to put all our efforts on landing the next job. I've spent several years getting more proficient at preparing and interviewing for real estate roles and the following are my insights for capitalizing on your female strengths so you can land your next job while wearing beautiful designer heels.

The Air Up There

Commercial real estate is an incredible, exciting industry that has been dominated by men and their sons for generations. According to the International Council of Shopping Centers (ICSC, 2014), the membership in the mid 2010s is still three to one, men to women. Women are most prevalent in the asset management roles and are least represented in the sales or leasing sector (Crew Network, 2007), which is commonly referred to as "deal making."

I've been a successful female deal maker for twenty-two years, but like so many women in the industry, I started out as a real estate coordinator overseeing the asset management for a growing brand. I was fortunate to find a manager who taught me how to negotiate rental reductions for existing locations and eventually let me try a deal making role.

I've always left one job for another with better pay, bigger deals, and a more impressive title. But when the economic crisis hit, I found myself unemployed and hunting for a new job. Unfortunately, most retail and restaurant chains discontinue new unit growth when sales are down or flat, so there were not many available jobs. The applicants lining up for these roles were impressively skilled, with long and diverse careers. I had to differentiate myself from the crowd.

Altitude Check

I went to the prescribed networking events and brushed up on my long since abandoned interviewing preparation and organization. The startling thing I learned and then experienced first hand was simple yet disturbing: hiring managers tend to hire in their own image, particularly in an economic downturn. And almost all of the hiring managers were men.

I don't think this practice is intentional, but rather the path of least resistance for the hiring manager. It is easier to hire someone who looks like you and has your same background. A younger version of yourself will duplicate the success you had when you were in the deal making role and will require minimal training. This is habitual and human and common.

And not the best news if you are a woman interviewing for a deal making role.

The good news is I had been successful for two decades and had a decent reputation and a succession of promotions to show for my efforts; this got me in the door for interviews on a regular basis. Once in that door, I had to represent myself the way I would represent this group once I had the job. So I rolled up my sleeves and went to work like a woman after a clearly defined target.

Pre-Flight

Job search and deal making require attention to detail and women excel at this! I put this specific skill into a thorough approach for the administrative portion of the interview preparation. It really is similar to compiling information on a potential real estate site you want to put before the real estate committee. All the paperwork has to be buttoned up and every foreseeable question asked, answered, and on a handy piece of paper at your side when you are seated before the hiring manager. Take the time to use your attention to detail and organizational skills to completely prepare for that interview.

Download all you can about the brand, including the timeline, the history and the ownership. Zero in on the individuals you will be meeting and the development plans and growth potential for the brand. Find people from within your network that have worked for or with someone on the development team and get the real story from them. Go visit their stores or restaurants and talk to the managers about their business. Invest time into understanding their brand and how this role you're interested in will contribute to their business.

I truly believe women have an advantage for the preparation portion of the process. In addition to the detailed approach, let your creative skills give you a distinctive edge. Remember the glittery posters you made in grade school and the elaborate pages for your son's scrapbook? The following is how I put my creative skills to work for my face-to-face interviews.

As soon as the interview was scheduled, I'd create a file folder that included their corporate logo on the tab. The logo is easy to find on the Internet. Is this overkill? Probably. The majority of the interviewers never noticed the detail but some of them had a favorable comment. It made me feel organized and professional. More importantly it showed the employer that I had already invested time and effort into this company and into this opportunity. Women are enthusiastic and creative. Don't underestimate the importance of conveying this! Remember, employees who are engaged and loyal to their brand are much more likely to be top performers. The hiring manager is looking to hire someone who *really wants* this job and putting a logo on a page is an easy way to show your heightened interest and set you apart from the other candidates.

Your file should contain all the downloaded documents that pertain to the hiring company's real estate growth, typed recaps of the phone interviews or previous HR screening sessions, materials found on the earnings and sales projections of the brand, and maps that show the locations of the existing units. It also contains all the data on you: resume copies, references, your list of deals you've done by brand and by state, and any articles you have written or that contain a quote of yours.

Once the background data is in place, it is time to prepare for your interview questions. Create a separate page for each person you will be speaking to face to face. Below the logo and name on each interviewer's page add their business profile from LinkedIn, which you can cut and paste. This should include their university and former employment. This information can give you a great entry question to break the ice. Below the profile is the list of questions crafted specifically for each interviewer. Sample questions include:

- Ask the head of HR, *"What does career progression look like for this role? How important is this in filling the position today?"*

- Ask the construction team, *"What are the biggest challenges for a deal maker in regard to the design of the physical site or facility?"*

- Ask the president or CFO, *"What is the most important contribution from the deal makers? What should be avoided?"*

- Ask a peer, *"What will be my biggest challenge in this role? What would you change if you were the CEO?"*

- Ask the head of development, *"How is the opening budget projected? Does the deal maker have input? What are the historical consequences if the goals are or are not met?"*

- Ask the hiring manager, *"Are there concerns about my candidacy that we have not yet addressed? What are the next steps in the hiring process?"*

Make sure you take notes on the page. This will help with your thank-you notes and for your on-boarding during the first few months of employment.

Taxi and Take-Off

Your face-to-face interview is now scheduled, and your research is complete and ready to be put to use. Now . . . what to wear? You want to look professional, conservative and almost borderline boring. Do not wear anything overly girly or trendy. Nothing low cut or too tight. *This* is not how you want to stand out! Wear a pant suit, button down or shell and of course your sensible heels. Recognize that some people are allergic to perfumes so do not use any on an interview day. The key is to dress like a confident woman who already works for the brand.

Remember to arrive early and if there is time, pre-drive the route so you know how long this will take you as well as where you should park, etc. Check your notes for the names of the administrators you have spoken to thus far in the process and greet them by name when you meet them. You want everybody pulling for you to be part of their team!

Be prepared for the common interview behavior-based questions and have great examples ready that will highlight your strengths and emphasize the attributes that will be important for this role. For example:

Q: *"Tell me about a difficult decision that positively influenced the outcome on a major project."*

A: Talk about getting a previous real estate committee comfortable with a site you felt strongly about. Speak to the process you went through, how you were able to influence the lead decision makers to a favorable outcome, and how the sales at the unit perform today. Be specific, genuine and current. Pick a success story you are most proud of and that is a site the industry knows performs well. Don't use an example of a steak house deal you did in the 1990s. Go back only two to three years at the most unless you are asked specifically about something from another era.

When the time comes, ask your questions with confidence and take notes. Don't be afraid to ask about next steps in the process. You want to consistently convey your interest in this role. But, most importantly, once you get to the table for your interview, enjoy yourself! Talk about the great work you have done and the hard fought deals you stole from the competition. You are your own VP of marketing! Flaunt your stuff!

The follow-up to the face-to-face interview used to be a hand written letter. Interviewers today are often away on business travel and letter mailboxes are not checked as often as they used to be. A thoughtful and timely email is now the preferred method of interview follow-up. Sloppy handwriting and errors in spelling and grammar can be avoided if your note is written electronically. This also gets your name back in front of the brand within hours of the interview.

Make sure your email has some follow up from what you talked about in the interview. Use your notes to help trigger what was discussed. For example, if you were speaking with the head of design about a new prototype that is down the street, go see it and comment on it in the follow up email. It is appropriate to send an email to every person who interviewed you face-to-face. Women have excellent follow up skills and there is no reason to skip this step. It just may set you apart from the other candidates.

Navigating the Air

The waiting is the hardest part! You nail the interview, you call your loved ones and glowingly recap your answers, you smile when you pass the retailer or restaurant every day and yet your phone is not ringing.

And the communication is so frustrating. Next week means next month. In the next quarter means maybe yet this year. Next fiscal budget means we've wasted your time. And you'd be surprised how many successful companies will spend big dollars on multiple meetings and expensive third party assessments for positions they don't end up filling. It can be maddening.

One of the components to interviewing for a corporate job this time around that wasn't at all prevalent two decades ago is the use of third party assessments. There are personality quizzes online, timed financial and problem solving exercises, and third party interviews done via Skype or FaceTime. Hiring managers want to put the last two to three candidates through some extra measures to insure they are focusing on the very best people for the role and to help determine which one of the finalists is the strongest candidate. These extra assignments are time consuming but it is important to work them into your schedule. Know that these cost the hiring company big dollars, so take the extra time commitment as an understanding that your candidacy warrants this additional monetary investment. You are on the short list of candidates moving forward.

Turbulence

Sometimes you get far along in a process and you think everything is going well when you learn bad news. Perhaps a candidate who turned them down a year ago is back interested. Perhaps they've decided the successful candidate needs to live in another city. Perhaps a previous employee wants to come back. Perhaps the hiring budget has been put on hold. Perhaps someone from the C-suite knows of someone else they used to work with at a previous company who'd be great. *You just never know.*

But when you get bad news you have to remain professional and thank them for their time. It is appropriate to send the hiring manager a follow up email saying *"While I am disappointed in the outcome, I am appreciative of the opportunity to get to know you. I remain interested in being a part of your team.*" You will want to stay connected to every hiring manager you've met because you never know when they may be building a team at another brand and you want to be at the top of that list as well. Women are excellent at keeping communication open and networking in place. We know not to burn a bridge. You just never know when the tide will rise.

Take Your Seat for Landing

You've finally got an offer in hand! While you are thrilled with it, you also recognize there are some components to it that you need (or you really want) to be tweaked. It is appropriate to negotiate these terms in a professional way and without drama or aggression. Use statements like *"I want to be part of your team but I will need a little more money than this to make this work for me financially. How can we sweeten this pot a little bit to get me closer to the number I need?"* Represent yourself well and don't be shy about asking for the outcome that is most favorable for you.

When you've got your final deal in hand, it is time to resign from your existing position. This is tough! Most women are empathetic and this skill serves you well when delivering hard news. My advice is to keep your sentences simple and direct. Stick to the facts and outline the timing.

Frequent Flyer

Even though you have replaced your position and moved on, it is beneficial to continue to stay in touch with hiring managers and continually network. You *never* know when you have impressed a hiring manager and they will call you about a role.

I've talked to many brands about deal making roles and have enjoyed the experience, even though it was maddening at times. I consider it great practice for the real thing. *And you never know when the thing will be real!* You have to put everything you've got into the process each time even if it means disappointment and heartbreak.

The outcome will eventually lean in your favor, but it may not be the path you thought it would take. Maybe the role you really wanted is at a chain that suddenly had to downsize and lay everyone off. Maybe the hiring manager will refer you to another excellent opportunity. Maybe the interviewer moves to another growing brand and is building a high performing team he will consider you for. Maybe another head count is added to the development budget and you get called back (grab your file!).

What I discovered and want you to know is that you can put your creative, organized, multi-tasking, over-communicating, highly developed, female skills toward finding a new job, and land it successfully! Utilizing your female skill set will make the process more enjoyable and the outcome sweeter.

All good landings are sweet and, ultimately, they take you home. Godspeed.

About Lisa Walker

Lisa Walker has over twenty-two years of real estate experience. She is the Director of Real Estate for the Corner Bakery Cafe, a fast casual bakery cafe with 170 units and franchise agreements signed for hundreds more.

Prior to joining Corner Bakery Cafe she led the development of Which Wich Superior Sandwiches where she was responsible for overseeing the new unit development of over two hundred restaurants during the critical years of growth for that brand. She also served as the National Director of Real Estate for Wendy's Hamburgers and led the deal making team and asset managers for twelve years.

She holds a BS in Organizational Communication from the University of Texas and is a former member of the original dance drill team, the world famous Kilgore College Rangerettes. She is an active member of ICSC, a Volunteer of the Year for the Women's Foodservice Forum, a Rangerette Forever and an active member in a professional DFW women's real estate group, Deals in Heels.

LinkedIn: LinkedIn.com/in/lisaawalker

Chapter 17

Swimming with the Big Fish
by Tina Wolfe

They told me this would be easy and once I began writing the words would flow, but I am not very optimistic since this is my first sentence and I have no idea where this is going. I will admit I am a procrastinator, but tend to work well under pressure . . . it's a Capricorn trait and those of you who are goats will understand. My ideas usually come at the most inconvenient time, mostly in the middle of the night when a keyboard or pen and paper is not readily available. I think this comes from having raised two children most of it as a single mother when the only time we have to ourselves seems to be when we are sleeping. So being the procrastinator that I am, I still don't know where this is going and what real estate topic I will end up covering, so hang in here with me and let's see where this goes. We women all know that commercial real estate is a male dominated industry and we women have decided we would like a piece of the pie. This brings me to what will be my chosen topic, *"Breaking into the Boys Club."*

I would like to tell you a story about my first year attending the largest real estate show held each year in Las Vegas (we all know which one that is).

First let me tell you a little bit about myself and my background. I am a feisty, somewhat fearless five foot, four inch, blonde haired, blue eyed woman. I came from the Food and Beverage industry where gender doesn't much matter as it is all about salesmanship. I was in the food industry for twenty-five years mostly working for others and then owning my own restaurant and dessert company. I ran the food and beverage department of a private Tennis Club and then for five years managed a country club with two eighteen hole golf courses, member dining, pool facilities and a full catering department. Trust me I know how to deal with all kinds of people. In 2000 I went through a divorce and had a five year old daughter and eight year old son to raise. I decided the long hours were not worth the time I was missing out on with my children...so I quit. I took four months off to regain my health and spend a lot of one on one time with my kids. My ex-husband and I have remained friends and have been pretty successful at co-parenting our children. When we were married he worked for a large hair care product company headquartered in our home town of El Paso. The CEO of the company just happened to have a commercial real estate company he started as a hobby which grew over time and is now one of the largest retail strip center developers in our town. They had a leasing job open... mind you I had no real estate experience, but my catering commissions were running out, the kids were on track and it was time to find a job. My ex-husband mentioned to the CEO that I was looking for a job and thought I would be a good fit. I dusted off my suit and went for an interview. The interview went well, but I was taken aback by one particular question I was asked. The CEO of this very large company asked me who would be taking care of the children; mind you, that type of question is illegal to ask any potential employee, but I laughed and told him their father would share the responsibility of childcare. Then he laughed and said they had other candidates to interview, but would let me know in a few weeks. Two weeks later, on a Friday, I received a call from the Director of Real Estate asking me if I could start the following Monday, and that on my first day I would be flying to Las Vegas for the real estate show. The following Monday I was packed and stepping onto a private jet to start my new career. Not a bad way to start a new job!

This brings us back to my first real estate show in Las Vegas. I had no idea what I was doing, but I thought this can't be too hard its sales and I have been selling all my life. I am a people person and I thought this can't be too different from running a restaurant and convincing people to try something new. I arrived at the convention center and ladies let me tell you, I had never seen so many suits in all my life. It was 2004 and the real estate market was on fire and every young, fresh out of college frat boy was there trying to prove themselves. My son who is in a fraternity would cringe if he heard me using the word frat and would quickly correct me with "Mom, its fraternity," but none the less the convention floor still looked like a huge frat party. In a sense the commercial real estate industry is somewhat like a fraternity or as we ladies call it "The Boys Club." I made my way through the convention center trying to keep up with my new boss and take in the sites. Since I wasn't sure what to bring I brought everything but the pair of flats I soon discovered were necessary, but I sure did look good in my suit and three inch heels. We talked to a lot of people and yet we didn't make one sale or should I say lease one square foot of space to anyone. I thought to myself, *"This is stupid. Why doesn't anyone want to buy what we had to sell? I can sell anything and this doesn't seem to be working. I must be doing something wrong."* By the end of the day my feet were permanently a part of my shoe and I didn't dare take them off for fear of never getting them back on. I lost my boss in the crowd and finally had a chance to go it alone and see what I could do, but of course I had no idea what I was doing. Most retailers were very kind and did a lot of smiling and sent me on my way with their business card in hand. I think they probably laughed once I was out of sight. After nine hours on my feet I finally boarded the shuttle bus back to my hotel to prepare for the round of diner and drinks with co-workers and potential clients. As luck would have it there was not a single seat left on that bus, but waiting for the next bus was not an option. As I stood in the isle and the bus began to pull away I realized that out of the seventy or so people on the bus only about one percent of those were women. This was the moment of truth; surely one of these gentlemen would remember the manners they were taught as young boys and offer their seat to a woman with swollen feet. At that precise moment I realized gender played no role in their decision making process; after all, they had the same grueling day I had, except for the heels. I was now considered competition and why would they make it any easier for me to be comfortable. As they frantically checked their phones for emails and text messages I thought, *"Boy, this is going to be cut throat."* It was time to put my big girl panties on and show them what I was made of so I thought to myself, "bring it on" because I am not a quitter and I hate to lose. I needed to think of what my strategy would be, it was after all like playing a monopoly game and I wasn't going to give up any of my property and I wanted to collect every time I passed "GO." Never doubt the determination of a woman; especially when her feet hurt and boy did they hurt!

After an evening of food and drink I came back to my room and did some homework. I mapped out my strategy, and the next day I hit the floor of the convention center with a new attitude. I was determined I was going to be taken seriously and I meticulously made the rounds. Here are a few of the lessons I learned that day that I would like to pass on:

- Pack as little as possible in your brief case, but always make room for those flats or flip flops.

- If you want to talk to a retailer at the Vegas show, you have to have made an appointment two to three months in advance of the show. If you don't have an appointment, I found that if you arrive as soon as the doors open to the convention center you can sometimes catch them before they start their scheduled appointments.

- Know what their criteria is and be as brief as possible leaving all pertinent information , which is easier said than done.

- They hate to lug back lots of paper so prepare an aerial with one, three, and five-mile radius rings highlighting acreages, existing retailers in the area, especially their competitors and demographic information.

- Leave them with a flash drive (easy to fly home with) containing all of the information you didn't have time to discuss in your ten-minute allotted time slot.

- Don't forget to get their card or contact information.

- Follow up with an email immediately upon returning home or even better on your plane ride home. Don't let up there because unless you are lucky enough to work in the major markets it can sometimes take years to close a deal.

If you want to succeed in the commercial real estate business you have to be patient and persistent and do your homework. Persistence brings to mind a story. One of my first retail targets to bring to El Paso was an Asian fast food concept and I religiously stopped by their booth in Las Vegas and Dallas for four years straight trying to convince them they needed to be in El Paso. I would show them sites and put fancy packages together and ask them why if they were in Albuquerque wouldn't it be logical that their next location be in El Paso? They would tell me every time *"We just don't understand that market Tina."* To say the least I was frustrated, but I stayed in touch with the regional real estate director throughout the years and finally while visiting with him in Dallas for the fourth year in a row he said to me *"Tina, we are getting closer to looking at El Paso and because you have been so persistent you will be the first person we call."* The fifth year began and low and behold they were ready to make their move into the El Paso market and guess who they called first? I finally had my chance to finalize a ground lease with them when suddenly they restructured their entire real estate department and the deal went cold. By then it was 2007 and everyone was beginning to see a shift in the market, little did we know what was about to happen to our industry and every other hard working American. As the market began to rise from the ashes so did the ground lease, but by that time I had decided to move to another company where I had a chance to learn about development and I was itching to learn more. I knew I had played an instrumental role in getting that store to the market. That company now has several stores and loves the El Paso market. The lesson is persistence pays off; it just takes time, sometimes a lot of time!

I learned a lot in the four years, but sometimes you have to move on to move up, and I had just about worn the curve out of that learning curve. I was very grateful for the knowledge I had gained, but somehow you just know when it's time to leave. My new position was with a development company that was expanding by leaps and bounds on a national level, and I wanted a seat on the bus. I had been at my new position for just under a year when all hell broke loose due to the mortgage crisis. I found myself on a March morning sitting at my desk as human resources moved throughout the offices with pink slips and boxes for the belongings of those being laid off. At noon that day all layoffs had been completed, and I found myself the lone survivor of my department. We now refer to it as "Black Friday," and every March we have a brief moment of terror when that dreadful date comes around, but the company is growing and hopefully there will be an opportunity for more women to move up in the ranks. I have now surpassed my five-year mark and have managed to learn a lot about development. As long as I can continue to learn something new and amazing then I will stay put, but moving up is just as important because it allows you to continue to learn and take on more responsibility. It is a mutual benefit to both employee and employer.

Four years ago I met these amazing women who have inspired me and have played a big part in my success as a woman in real estate. We women are sometimes our own worst enemies, and I have no patience for those of my gender who step on others to move up the corporate ladder. Yet it becomes powerful to gather with a group of women of all different ages and at different stages of their careers, who strive to help each other. Madeleine Albright said, *"There is a special place in hell for women who don't help other women."* I can't imagine what that looks like. I have an amazing daughter and son, but I know my daughter will have a much tougher time in her career because she is a female, but if she is surrounded by an amazing group of women as I am she will conquer the world. Don't get me wrong I have met a significant number of men who have been exceptional mentors, but that sisterhood can't be beat. If

I can give any advice I would tell you this, find other women in the real estate business, young or new to the business you feel would benefit from your mentoring and make it a point of taking them under your wing. I would be nothing without the women who took the time to mentor me. We have amazing minds and when we bond them altogether amazing things can happen.

So as I stepped on that bus last year after eight hours of nonstop walking and talking to head back to my hotel I found the last available seat and watched as several more men and women boarded. The bus pulled away with several men and women standing in the aisle just as it had four years ago when I boarded. I waited and watched to see if anything had changed, and low and behold someone remembered what their mothers and fathers had taught them so long ago . . . chivalry wasn't dead after all. As a mother I was proud of that young man who stood and offered his seat to the young lady standing in the aisle. I wanted to tell his mother she had done a good job and that I hoped my son was doing the same. Don't forget, we raise the men of this world. How powerful is that?

So as I prepare to head back to Vegas this year and as I look across that convention floor I hope to see a steady flow of women beaming with confidence, heels on, flip flops protruding from their bags. I find great satisfaction in helping other women and I for one don't want to see that special hell, so I will continue the work so many women before me started, and I will pass that along to my daughter, and she to her daughter.

This has been a phenomenal opportunity for me and for everyone involved in this project and I feel very much empowered and look forward to meeting all of the authors. Keep it up ladies you are awesome!

About Tina Wolfe

Tina Wolfe was born in New Orleans, Louisiana and moved to El Paso, Texas where she's been in the commercial real estate industry for ten years. She's currently the Commercial Sales Manager for Hunt Development Group in El Paso, Texas. She was previously in the Food and Beverage industry for twenty years, owning her own restaurant and dessert company. She has professional training in the Culinary Arts. Tina has two children, a son and daughter who both attend The University of Denver, which is the reason she works so hard.

Facebook: Facebook.com/DealsandHeelsTinaWolfe

Chapter 18

How to Get a Rent Reduction
by an Anonymous Commercial
Real Estate Professional

The key to successfully negotiating a real estate deal, or any deal for that matter, is all in the preparation. I estimate, not by any big survey, but just based upon personal experience, more than eighty to ninety percent of the work is done on the front-end of a transaction. This work needs to be done before you ever pick up the phone to discuss a deal. Fact finding and research is king in this world and the more information you can obtain to substantiate your (or your clients) position, the better off you will be.

First, start with the basics of your location. I am most involved in commercial real estate, with a special focus in retail, but have experience in all product types from office, industrial and even the multi-family arena. Although all different types of real estate transactions have a lot of similarities, the negotiation tactics to each type of property and their approach are very different.

So for this exercise, I will focus on one product type, retail, and how to approach the merits of a location. If you are negotiating a lease for yourself or one of your clients, you must arm yourself with as much pertinent information specific to that location and business as possible. You will need to know current sales, and how they are trending for the last several years, customer counts, and how those have changed. You need to know what portion of the business is now over the Internet, and what percentage that has increased over the years. If any of these trends were to continue, what would sales of the brick and mortar location potentially look like at the end of the new lease term, and question whether your client should lock themselves into a long-term lease.

Then you need to educate yourself on the actual site. Is this site a prototypical location for this concept? Does it have too much square footage or not enough? Is the shopping center fully occupied or does it have lots of space available? Does the shopping center or anchor tenant drive customers to your tenants business? Is there a neighboring shopping center that might be a better location? Does your client have good access, great visibility, and pylon signage to advertise their business? These are all questions you need to consider and be prepared to discuss and present to the owner of the shopping center.

A formal survey of the site is usually very helpful for taking notes. This survey should have the property name and address and a list of approximately fifteen items for you to answer. The items to be included are as follows—signage—is it adequate or smaller than others? Does your tenant have a panel on the shopping center pylon? How is the visibility to the site? Can you see it from the major intersection or is it more hidden? How is the access during peak times? Is it easy to get in and out of or more difficult? Who are the anchor tenants in the Shopping Center, and are they likely to be long-term good tenants who help your client's business? Who are other surrounding tenants and do they also contribute to the success of your client? How is the parking—is there ample parking for your client's customers or are spaces taken during peak times? Is there high turn-over and vacancy in the shopping center? Who are your client's competition and do they have a better location than their competition, or are they out-positioned by the competition? All of this information is key to understand and consider.

Next, you want to look at market rental rates. The best way to do this if you haven't done a transaction in the immediate trade area before, is to cold-call the landlord or listing agent for the property you or your client is located in, and ask what the going lease rates are and what type of incentives they are offering. This usually works if you explain you have a tenant who is potentially interested in leasing space in their center or one of the competing centers. It is always good to know their asking rates and you can usually assume they will come off those rates, at least slightly, once a formal offer is submitted. So you should discount them accordingly. No one ever quotes their bottom line price over the phone.

You also want to find out what other transactions have been completed or recently renewed, this information may be more difficult to obtain. This is where networking usually comes in handy. If you are actively networking in your field, you should have connections of some sort to be able to confirm information. This network could include other real estate brokers who may have completed a transaction in the center, or other real estate reps from national tenants who could give you the latest information on their location. Most of the time, if you have information to give them, they will reciprocate. A local broker might want to know what your client is paying, and therefore, be more apt to disclose the rent they were able to negotiate. Most of the time, brokers are not bound to confidentiality agreements, but sometimes that can be the case.

After you have gathered all the facts about the business and the trends, as well as the market rental rates, then you need to research the surrounding retail properties. The best thing to do is to identify a potential relocation site or sites. Call each of those options and get proposals to lease new space from those centers. It is very likely in today's market place, you might have some very aggressive landlord's who want you or your retail client to move to their location. They may offer more aggressive rental rates and lots of incentives to get you to move. This could come in the form of free rent, tenant improvement allowances and even moving allowances. A good broker needs to analyze and consider all the expenses and incentives to get to a new net effective rental rent.

Finally, after all this research is complete, spend time on the strategy of your negotiations. How are you going to achieve a rent reduction? What is the angle you are going to use to convince the property owner that you must have a rent reduction in order to renew this location? What must your client get to stay at the same profitability for next year? The angle and the believability is extremely important in these negotiations. What are all the negatives of this specific location? Are sales down from last year? Is traffic decreased into your store? Has more of your business moved to the Internet? Could you get a better deal if you moved across the street to the other shopping center? Does the property have a great anchor for your business? What is *your* angle? Whatever the angle or angles are, be prepared to discuss it in great detail by giving specific information for this location. For example, it is much more powerful and believable if you state that sales are down 7.5 percent from last year and despite cutting some part-time staff, profits are lagging by more than sixteen percent. You can then tell the landlord, in order to maintain the location, you have to have an equal amount of rent reduction. And speaking of believability, you must believe you can do this otherwise you will never be able to convince anyone else.

Once I had an employee who always seemed to be at the bottom of the group in achieving rent reductions. She had a good market to achieve rent relief for our business because she was in Louisiana versus Manhattan, but she always struggled. Turns out she never believed she could get one and always ended up taking the landlord position when explaining why rent was going up. This always comes through when negotiating. If you don't have strong arguments and a believe yourself, it is almost impossible to convince anyone else.

Speaking of believing, you need to pick your strong most believable argument. A good way to determine the best argument or angle is to write all the information down, *both* negatives and positives. Pick the negative one that is most compelling but have several of the other negative facts to throw in. After you have determined the best angle and set a target price—shoot lower. If you believe a ten percent reduction would be a good win, ask for a twenty percent reduction, because that will leave you room to negotiate. And many times, believe it or not, you may get what you ask for! Remember if you don't ask for it, you won't get it. Lists are key. You might be thinking, why would I need to write down positives? We need to be aware of the positives too, that way when the landlord brings them up, we are prepared to agree but then remind them of all the negatives and how they might outweigh the positives.

And finally . . . after you've done all this work, it's time to pick up the phone for the first time! By now, you should truly be prepared. I recommend dealing with the decision maker in the process, if possible. Anyone relaying your message won't do it very effectively. When making contact for the first time, explain you are representing their tenant XYZ, and you are currently reviewing all options for them which include relocating their business. If this isn't believable, use the best angle you came up with. As an example, your client may occupy 1,200 more square feet than they really need, but they are willing to consider staying in the current space at a slight rent reduction. This sets the stage for the negotiations to begin. Whatever angle or angles you have explain them in detail. If the latest prototype location is 2,000 square feet, and this location is 3,200 square feet, that is very powerful information. Talk in terms of dollars too, suggesting that it is costing your client an extra $23,000 per year ($20 + $3 in triple nets X 1,200) in unneeded expense for this location. This in turn, is driving down the profitability of this specific location. On your first call, it is also very important to make friends with the landlord. Having a good rapport is important and being able to connect on a positive personal level can be very helpful.

I remember negotiating a transaction in Huntington Beach, CA. The landlord lived in Del Ray, and sounded about one-hundred years old on the phone. He indicated he would be happy to discuss the transaction, but always did better in person, and could I come to his home and meet with him? Now normally, I wouldn't recommend this, but I was thirty-seven at the time, so I thought I could handle a one-hundred year old if there were any trouble! Turns out he was only ninety-seven. Truly, I think he just wanted the company. We visited about my client, talked about their business, discussed the awesome almost iconic site he had, but how difficult it would be to re-lease because it was too large for most users (including my client) and very difficult to subdivide. He then asked if we could meet for dinner and discuss it further, that he thought I was making good points, but wanted to solve everything over a glass of wine. I remember thinking the last thing I really wanted to do was go to dinner with a ninety-seven year old while traveling in LA, but thought if I did, I'd probably be able to conclude the negotiations. So, I took one for my client, and agreed to meet ninety-seven for dinner. It was a lovely dinner and I got to hear some truly fascinating stories about his travels and how he acquired property over the years. Most importantly, we were able to resolve our differences and agreed upon a reasonable rent, which ended up being only a slight reduction. However, if I hadn't had met with this landlord in person, I'm certain the rent would have been at least a ten percent increase. This is why it is so important to establish a relationship.

It always helps to make friends with the landlord. The old saying, you catch more flies with honey than vinegar applies here. Ensure the landlord you are trying to help them keep the tenant in their current location and you are looking to secure a long-term lease which maybe in their best interest, given the current market conditions. This usually resonates with most property owners. Explain that in order to secure a long-term lease though, you need to rectify the current situation and a rent reduction must happen. At this point, do not get into specific numbers, only state all the negatives of the property and tell them you will send them a proposal for their review and consideration. You realize the landlord will need to think about their tenant's situation, but hopefully you have made them understand the position they are currently facing. If the landlord presses you for what you want over the phone, tell them you have not nailed down numbers yet because there are two other properties under consideration.

Many good brokers make the mistake of not sending a formal LOI at this point. A great broker or good Transaction Manger will always send a formal LOI. This gives you the opportunity to reiterate the problems with the current business and location—which you have already explained over phone—and outlines the specific transaction you believe the tenant will accept. Restate what is wrong with this location and a few of the negative items you previously discussed. It is an important document that needs to be used not only to avoid any confusion of what was agreed upon, but you have to spend time crafting the opening paragraph reinforcing the position of the tenant. Always thank the landlord for their time, but remind them the tenant has a lot of options in today's marketplace.

Another key to successful negotiations is to start very early in the process. If you start too late, the landlord may know you don't have time to execute a move to another center. And if they realize this, you may not get a rent reduction; you may likely get a rent increase! Therefore, start early, twelve to eighteen months ahead of the option notice date in the lease is recommended. Because you are asking for a reduction and that's not an easy decision for the property owner, it will take time to convince the landlord. A typical negotiation usually takes place over four to six conversations and three to four rounds going over the letter of intent. If you have only spoken once or twice, you probably haven't tried hard enough.

In Retail, most of the time the old adage applies—location, location, location. And therefore, many times it is very difficult to relocate a retail business. However, you have to convince a landlord you won't hesitate to recommend a relocation given today's increased environment with Internet sales. Some businesses could spend the money they would have on rent, to advertise their business on the Internet and potentially come out ahead. It is your job to find these facts and educate the landlord on your client's business. Maybe your client's business is an ice cream shop that is well located next to a busy movie theater, so you think you have no credible argument regarding Internet sales. What do you do then? What other factors may come into play for this business? Maybe there was a new bakery that opened down the block that offers ice cream cakes too, and this represented more than ten percent of your client's sales. So, you may have not been able to use any Internet angles for this example, but there is almost always another angle to take, you just need to do the research to uncover the information.

One thing I would never recommend is to ask for a proposal from the landlord. Many brokers make this mistake because it may be easier for them, and it puts the ball into someone else's court. However, this is usually a big mistake when representing retail tenants. In a retail property, if you ask for a proposal from the landlord, the proposal is likely going to have an increase in rent. If the landlord suggests a higher rate, you will be fighting against that higher rate and working to try to keep your clients rental rate flat, at best case. However, if you submit the first offer, you will be asking for a rent reduction, and the landlord will be fighting against your number. This usually makes it easier to get to your target reduction number.

Negotiating a lease can be a very fun challenge, and when you prepare as suggested, I have no doubt you will get great results for your clients. And when you get great results for your clients, you get more business from them and their referrals. You will reap the rewards. Always focus on the client and never worry about how much commission you will or will not make. If you always keep your clients interest at heart, you will succeed.

Chapter 19
Bonus
Pam Goodwin's
26 Lessons Learned from
26 Years in Commercial Real Estate

by Pamela J. Goodwin

1. Find the right mentor/boss/company. Work only for people you enjoy being around.

2. Learn something new every day. Listen to audio tapes in the car instead of the radio. I enjoy listening to Zig Ziglar tapes.

3. Suggest working for a landlord, tenant and brokerage firm to gain the experience from different viewpoints.

4. Get involved in your national and regional organizations (ICSC, NTCAR, CREW)—serve on a committee.

5. Attend networking events in commercial real estate and outside your industry—always be the first person to show up and carry a genuine smile on your face.

6. Join or start a women-only commercial real estate organization in your city and meet once a month with keynote speakers. Meet for lunch the same day each month. For example, pick the last Tuesday of each month at the same time of day.

7. Obtain your sales and broker's license in your state. Always be taking classes.

8. Have coffee or lunch with a person in the business whom you look up to and respect. Send them a letter and let them know how much you would like to meet with them. You will be surprised how many will respond and meet with you. I always wanted to meet with Barbara Corcoran from Shark Tank. I researched and looked up her website and sent in a request for a private consultation. Guess what? We met for two hours in her New York City Park Avenue office to talk about business. It was a once in a life time experience.

9. Get to know your local and national writers for trade magazines, newspapers and articles—they are always looking for stories to write about for upcoming articles.

10. Help others find jobs—if you hear of an open position send it out to people you know may be looking.

11. Sell the sizzle—talk about the top three reasons to lease or sell a property. Be creative when promoting the property—don't be boring. When I was marketing a Twin Peaks property I used the words "scenic views" to get attention - and it did.

12. ABC's of Real Estate—Always Be Closing and Always Be Canvassing! Bottom line in real estate if you are not selling something you have nothing to close! You always have to have a pipeline of deals in the work.

13. People do business with people they trust and like. Find a common thing—college you went to, running 5k marathons, golfing, kids events, where you grew up, etc. Now you can look up the person on LinkedIn or their web site before you meet with them. Be prepared. People will be impressed if you take the time to get to know them a little bit. I always remember Larry King's quote, *"I never learned anything when I was doing the talking."*

14. Tell everyone your goals. People want to help people reach their goals.

15. Invite people over to your house so they can get to know you on a personal level.

16. If you don't know something learn it! Take a class; hire someone to show you, research on the Internet, etc. Take action!

17. You only have two things—time and Information—so do not give either of them away. Don't let time wasters distract you. Think like an attorney—the minute you call them the clock starts ticking for their information and you are being charged.

18. Persistence pays off. Don't give up too soon, but know when to move on. This can be difficult sometimes, but move on.

19. Pick up the phone. You can learn so much more when you talk to someone versus sending an email. Donald

Trump says if an email is over ten words you need to pick up the phone.

20. Ask for the order. People are not mind readers. You need to let them know you want their business.

21. Touch your prospects every day or someone else will. It typically takes seven different touches before you get a prospect's attention. Be creative. Send a company gift, invite them to a concert or sporting event, send a fax (no one does this anymore and most times your fax will be placed on the person's chair as important), deliver them lunch, etc.

22. Be the go-to person. Find a niche and know your stuff. Make sure you are the person they call first!

23. Give and take information. You learned this as a kid. Don't ever be the one who calls just to get the information and never shares information.

24. Be unique and memorable. What makes you stand out from the rest of the people in commercial real estate? What is your trademark—your suit colors, your hair, your smile, your special knowledge?

25. Fortune is in the follow-up. Most people do not follow up after meeting someone, or even when there is business.

26. Have fun! Life is too short not to do something you enjoy waking up every day to do.

Made in the USA
Middletown, DE
04 June 2021

41100894R00126